Encountering Shame and Guilt

Encountering Shame and Guilt

Resources
for Strategic Pastoral Counseling

Daniel Green and Mel Lawrenz

Baker Books

A Division of Baker Book House Co
Grand Rapids, Michigan 49516

146451

© 1994 by Daniel R. Green and Mel Lawrenz

Published by Baker Books,
a division of Baker Book House Company
P.O. Box 6287, Grand Rapids, Michigan 49516-6287

Printed in the United States of America

Library of Congress Cataloging-in-Publication Data

Green, Daniel (Daniel R.)
   Encountering shame and guilt/Daniel Green and Mel Lawrenz.
   p. cm.—(Resources for strategic pastoral counseling)
ISBN 0-8010-3863-4
   1. Pastoral counseling. 2. Shame—Religious aspects—Christianity. 3. Guilt—Religious aspects—Christianity. I. Lawrenz, Mel. II. Title. III. Series.
BV4012.2.G75   1993
253.5—dc20   93-40946

to our children
Melanie and David
Eva and Christopher

Contents

Acknowledgments

Long before any of the ideas in this book were committed to paper they were developed at length with our wives, Lynne and Ingrid. We found that guilt and shame were such fundamental human issues that reach into every aspect of life, that a pastor, a psychologist, an educator, and a social worker could discover almost endless applications and connections. The contents of this work, therefore, owe much to the creative work invested by our life partners.

It was a real privilege to be able to develop and test these ideas with our colleagues at New Life Resources, Inc., and Elmbrook Church. They know that guilt and shame are issues that come up in pastoral ministry or professional counseling almost every day. They are looking for good answers to the pressing questions we all have, and thus they helped us keep this work practical.

We are also thankful for the numerous contributions offered by the many Elmbrook Christian Study Center students who participated in a class titled "Guilt and Shame in Christian Perspective." Their insights, questions, and feedback sharpened our understanding and were much appreciated.

An Introduction to Strategic Pastoral Counseling

David G. Benner

W hile the provision of spiritual counsel has been an integral part of Christian soul care since the earliest days of the church, the contemporary understanding and practice of pastoral counseling is largely a product of the twentieth century. Developing within the shadow of the modern psychotherapies, pastoral counseling has derived much of its style and approach from these clinical therapeutics. What this has meant is that pastoral counselors have often seen themselves more as counselors than as pastors and the counseling that they have provided has often been a rather awkward adaptation of clinical counseling models to a pastoral context. This, in turn, has often resulted in significant tension between the pastoral and psychological dimensions of the counseling provided by clergy and others in Christian ministry. It is also frequently reflected in pastoral counselors who are more interested in anything connected with the modern mystery cult of psychotherapy than with their own tradition of Christian soul care, and who, as a consequence, are often quite insecure in their pastoral role and identity.

While pastoral counseling owes much to the psychological culture that has gained ascendancy in the West during the past cen-

11

tury, this influence has quite clearly been a mixed blessing. Contemporary pastoral counselors typically offer their help with much more psychological sophistication than was the case several decades ago, but all too often they do so without a clear sense of the uniqueness of counseling that is offered by a pastor. And not only are the distinctive spiritual resources of Christian ministry often deemphasized or ignored, but the tensions that are associated with attempts to directly translate clinical models of counseling into the pastoral context become a source of much frustration. This is in part why so many pastors report dissatisfaction with their counseling. While they indicate that this dissatisfaction is a result of insufficient training in and time for counseling, a bigger part of the problem may be that pastors have been offered approaches to counseling that are of questionable appropriateness for the pastoral context and that will inevitably leave them feeling frustrated and inadequate.

Strategic Pastoral Counseling is a model of counseling that has been specifically designed to fit the role, resources, and needs of the typical pastor who counsels. Information about this "typical" pastor was solicited by means of a survey of over 400 pastors (this research is described in the introductory volume of the series, *Strategic Pastoral Counseling: A Short-Term Structured Model* [Benner 1992]). The model appropriates the insights of contemporary counseling theory without sacrificing the resources of pastoral ministry. Furthermore, it takes its form and direction from the pastoral role and in so doing offers an approach to counseling that is not only congruent with the other aspects of pastoral ministry but that places pastoral counseling at the very heart of ministry.

The present volume represents an application of Strategic Pastoral Counseling to one commonly encountered problem situation. As such, it presupposes a familiarity with the basic model. Readers not familiar with *Strategic Pastoral Counseling: A Short-Term Structured Model* should consult this book for a detailed presentation of the model and its implementation. What follows is a brief review of this material which, while it does not adequately summarize all that is presented in that book, should serve as a reminder of the most important features of the Strategic Pastoral Counseling approach.

The Strategic Pastoral Counseling Model

Strategic Pastoral Counseling is short-term, bibliotherapeutic, wholistic, structured, spiritually focused, and explicitly Christian. Each of these characteristics will be briefly discussed in order.

Short-Term Counseling

Counseling can be brief (that is, conducted over a relatively few sessions), time-limited (that is, conducted within an initially fixed number of total sessions), or both. Strategic Pastoral Counseling is both brief and time-limited, working within a suggested maximum of five sessions. The decision to set this upper limit on the number of sessions was in response to the fact that the background research conducted in the design of the model indicated that 87 percent of the pastoral counseling conducted by pastors in general ministry involves five sessions or less. This short-term approach to counseling seems ideally suited to the time availability, training, and role demands of pastors.

Recent research in short-term counseling has made it clear that while such an approach requires that the counselor be diligent in maintaining the focus on the single agreed upon central problem, significant and enduring changes can occur through a very small number of counseling sessions. Strategic Pastoral Counseling differs, in this regard, from the more ongoing relationship of discipleship or spiritual guidance. In these, the goal is the development of spiritual maturity. Strategic Pastoral Counseling has a much more modest goal: examining a particular problem or experience in the light of God's will for and activity in the life of the individual seeking help and attempting to facilitate growth in and through that person's present life situation. While this is still an ambitious goal, its focused nature makes it quite attainable within a short period of time. It is this focus that makes the counseling strategic.

The five-session limit should be communicated by the pastor no later than the first session and preferably in the prior conversation when the time is set for this session. This ensures that the parishioner is aware of the time limit from the beginning and can share responsibility in keeping the counseling sessions focused. Some people will undoubtedly require more than five sessions in order to bring about a resolution of their problems. These people should be referred to someone who is appropriately qualified for such work; preparation for this referral will be one of the goals of the five sessions. However, the fact that such people may require more help than can be provided in five sessions of pastoral counseling does not mean that they cannot benefit from such focused short-term pastoral care; no individuals should be regarded as inappropriate candidates for Strategic Pastoral Counseling merely because they may require other help.

One final but important note about the suggested limit of five sessions is that this does not have to be tied to a corresponding period of five weeks. In fact, many pastors find weekly sessions to be less useful than sessions scheduled two or three weeks apart. This sort of spacing of the last couple of sessions is particularly helpful and should be considered even if the first several sessions are held weekly.

Bibliotherapeutic Counseling

Bibliotherapy refers to the therapeutic use of reading. Strategic Pastoral Counseling builds the use of written materials into the heart of its approach to pastoral caregiving. The Bible itself is, of course, a rich bibliotherapeutic resource and the encouragement of and direction in its reading is an important part of Strategic Pastoral Counseling. Its use must be disciplined and selective and particular care must be taken to ensure that it is never employed in a mechanical or impersonal manner. However, when used appropriately it can unquestionably be one of the most dynamic and powerful resources available to the pastor who counsels.

While the Bible is a unique bibliotherapeutic resource, it is not the only such resource. Strategic Pastoral Counseling comes with a built-in set of specifically designed resources. Each of the 10 volumes in this series has an accompanying book written for the parishioner who is being seen in counseling. These resource books are written by the same authors as the volumes for pastors and are designed for easy integration into counseling sessions.

The use of reading materials that are consistent with the counseling being provided can serve as a most significant support and extension of the counseling offered by a pastor. The parishioner now has a helping resource that is not limited by the pastor's time and availability. Furthermore, the pastor can now allow the written materials to do part of the work of counseling, using the sessions to deal with those matters that are not as well addressed through the written page.

Wholistic Counseling

It might seem surprising to suggest that a short-term counseling approach should also be wholistic. But this is both possible and highly desirable. Wholistic counseling is counseling that is responsive to the totality of the complex psycho-spiritual dynamics that make up the life of human persons. Biblical psychology is clearly a wholistic psychology. The various "parts" of persons (i.e., body, soul, spirit, heart, flesh, etc.) are never presented as separate faculties or independent components of persons but always as different ways of seeing the whole person. Biblical discussions of persons emphasize first and foremost their essential unity of being. Humans are ultimately understandable only in the light of this primary and irreducible wholeness and helping efforts that are truly Christian must resist the temptation to see persons only through their thoughts, feelings, behaviors, or any other single manifestation of being.

The alternative to wholism in counseling is to focus on only one of these modalities of functioning and this is, indeed, what many approaches to counseling do. In contrast, Strategic Pastoral Counseling asserts that pastoral counseling must be responsive to the behavioral (action), cognitive (thought), and affective (feeling) elements of personal functioning. Each examined separately can obscure that which is really going on with a person. But taken together they form the basis for a comprehensive assessment and effective intervention. Strategic Pastoral Counseling provides a framework for ensuring that each of these spheres of functioning is addressed and this, in fact, provides much of the structure for the counseling.

Structured Counseling

The structured nature of Strategic Pastoral Counseling is that which enables its brevity, ensuring that each of the sessions has a clear focus and that each builds upon the previous ones in contributing toward the accomplishment of the overall goals. The framework that structures Strategic Pastoral Counseling is sufficiently tight as to enable the pastor to provide a wholistic assessment and counseling intervention within a maximum of five sessions and yet it is also sufficiently flexible to allow for differences in individual styles of different counselors. This is very important because Strategic Pastoral Counseling is not primarily a set of techniques but an intimate encounter of and dialogue between people.

The structure of Strategic Pastoral Counseling grows out of the goal of addressing the feelings, thoughts, and behaviors that are part of the troubling experiences of the person seeking help. It is also a structure that is responsive to the several tasks that face the pastoral counselor, tasks such as conducting an initial assessment, developing a general understanding of the problem and of the person's major needs, and selecting and delivering interventions and resources that will bring help. This structure is described in more detail later.

Spiritually Focused Counseling

The fourth distinctive of Strategic Pastoral Counseling is that it is spiritually focused. This does not mean that only religious matters are discussed. Our spirituality is our essential heart commitments, our basic life direction, and our fundamental allegiances. These spiritual aspects of our being are, of course, reflected in our attitudes toward God and are expressed in our explicitly religious values and behaviors. However, they are also reflected in matters that may seem on the surface to be much less religious. Strategic Pastoral Counselors place a primacy on listening to this underlying spiritual story. They listen for what we might call the story behind the story.

But listening to the story behind the story requires that one first listen to and take seriously the presenting story. To disregard the presenting situation is spiritualization of a problem. It fails to take the problem seriously and makes a mockery of counseling as genuine dialogue. The Strategic Pastoral Counselor thus listens to and enters into the experience of parishioners as they relate their struggles and life's experiences. But while this is a real part of the story, it is not the whole story that must be heard and understood. For in the midst of this story emerges another: the story of their spiritual response to these experiences. This response may be one of unwavering trust in God but a failure to expect much of him. Or it may be one of doubt, anger, confusion, or despair. Each of these is a spiritual response to present struggles and in one form or another, the spiritual aspect of the person's experience will always be discernible to the pastor who watches for it. Strategic Pastoral Counseling makes this underlying spiritual story the primary focus.

Explicitly Christian Counseling

While it is important to not confuse spirituality with religiosity, it is equally important to not confuse Christian spirituality with any of its imitations. In this regard, it is crucial that Strategic Pastoral Counseling be distinctively and explicitly Christian. And while Strategic Pastoral Counseling begins with a focus on spiritual matters understood broadly, its master goal is to facilitate the other person's awareness of and response to the call of God to surrender and service. This is the essential and most important distinctive of Strategic Pastoral Counseling.

One of the ways in which Strategic Pastoral Counseling is made explicitly Christian is through its utilization of Christian theological language, images, and concepts and the religious resources of prayer, Scripture, and the sacraments. These resources must never be used in a mechanical, legalistic, or magical fashion. But used sensitively and wisely, they can be the conduit for a dynamic contact between God and the person seeking pastoral help. And this is the goal of their utilization, not some superficial baptizing of the counseling in order to make it Christian but rather a way of bringing the one seeking help more closely in touch with the God who is the source of all life, growth, and healing.

Another important resource that is appropriated by the Strategic Pastoral Counselor is that of the church as a community. Too often pastoral counseling is conducted in a way that is not appreciably different from that which might be offered by a Christian counselor in private practice. This most unfortunate practice ignores the rich resources that are potentially available in any Christian congregation. One of the most important ways in which Strategic Pastoral Counseling is able to maintain its short-term nature is by the pastor connecting the person seeking help with others in the church who can provide portions of that help. The congregation can, of course, also be involved in less individualistic ways. Support and ministry groups of various sorts are becoming a part of many congregations that seek to provide a dynamic ministry to their community and are potentially important resources for the Strategic Pastoral Counselor.

A final and even more fundamental way in which Strategic Pastoral Counseling is Christian is in the reliance that it encourages on the Holy Spirit. The Spirit is the indispensable source of all wisdom that is necessary for the practice of pastoral counseling. Recognizing that all healing and growth are ultimately of God, the Strategic Pastoral Counselor can thus take comfort in this reliance on the Spirit of God and on the fact that ultimate responsibility for people and their well-being lies with God.

Stages and Tasks of Strategic Pastoral Counseling

The three overall stages that organize Strategic Pastoral Counseling can be described as *encounter*, *engagement*, and *disengagement*. The first stage of Strategic Pastoral Counseling, encounter, corresponds to the initial session in which the goal is to establish personal contact with the person seeking help, set the boundaries for the counseling relationship, become acquainted with that person and the central concerns, conduct a pastoral diagnosis, and develop a mutually acceptable focus for the subsequent sessions. The second stage, engagement, involves the pastor moving beyond the first contact and establishing a deeper working alliance with the person seeking help. This normally occupies the next one to three sessions and entails the exploration of the person's feelings, thoughts, and behavioral patterns associated with this problem area and the development of new perspectives and strategies for coping or change. The third and final stage, disengagement, describes the focus of the last one or possibly two sessions, and involves an evaluation of progress and an assessment of remaining concerns, the making of a referral for further help if this is needed, and the ending of the counseling relationship. These stages and tasks are summarized in the table below.

Stages and Tasks of Strategic Pastoral Counseling

Stage 1:   Encounter (Session 1)
      * Joining and boundary-setting
      * Exploring the central concerns and relevant history
      * Conducting a pastoral diagnosis
      * Achieving a mutually agreeable focus for counseling

Stage 2:   Engagement (Sessions 2, 3, 4)
      * Exploration of cognitive, affective, and behavioral aspects of the problem and the identification of resources for coping or change

Stage 3:   Disengagement (Sessions 4, 5)
      * Evaluation of progress and assessment of remaining concerns
      * Referral (if needed)
      * Termination of counseling

The Encounter Stage

The first task in this initial stage of Strategic Pastoral Counseling is joining and boundary-setting. Joining involves putting the parishioner at ease by means of a few moments of casual conversation that is designed to ease pastor and parishioner into contact. Such preliminary conversation should never take more than five minutes and should usually be kept to two or three. It will not always be necessary, because some people are immediately ready to tell their story. Boundary-setting involves the communication of the purpose of this session and the time frame for the session and your work together. This should not normally require more than a sentence or two.

The exploration of central concerns and relevant history usually begins with an invitation for parishioners to describe what led them to seek help at the present time. After hearing an expression of these immediate concerns, it is usually helpful to get a brief historical perspective on these concerns and the person. Ten to 15 minutes of exploration of the course of development of the presenting problems and their efforts to cope or get help with them is the foundation of this part of the session. It is also important at this point to get some idea of the parishioner's present living and family arrangements as well as work and/or educational situation. The organizing thread for this section of the first interview should be the presenting problem. These matters will not be the only ones discussed but this focus serves to give the session the necessary direction.

Stripped of its distracting medical connotations, diagnosis is problem definition and this is a fundamental part of any approach to counseling. Diagnoses involve judgments about the nature of the problem and, either implicitly or explicitly, pastoral counselors make such judgments every time they commence a counseling relationship. But in order for diagnoses to be relevant they must guide the counseling that will follow. This means that the categories of pastoral assessment must be primarily related to the spiritual focus, which is foundational to any counseling that is appropriately called pastoral. Thus, the diagnosis called for in the first stage of Strategic Pastoral Counseling involves an assessment of the person's spiritual well-being.

The framework for pastoral diagnosis adopted by Strategic Pastoral Counseling is that suggested by Malony (1988) and used as the basis of his Religious Status Interview. Malony proposed that the diagnosis of Christian religious well-being should involve the assessment of the person's awareness of God, acceptance of God's grace, repentance and responsibility, response to God's leadership and direction, involvement in the church, experience of fellowship, ethics, and openness in the faith. While this approach to pastoral diagnosis has been found to be helpful by many, the Strategic Pastoral Counselor need not feel confined by it. It is offered as a suggested framework for conducting a pastoral assessment and each individual pastoral counselor needs to approach this task in ways that fit his or her own theological convictions and personal style. Further details on conducting a pastoral assessment can be found in *Strategic Pastoral Counseling: A Short-Term Structured Model.*

The final task of the encounter stage of Strategic Pastoral Counseling is achieving a mutually agreeable focus for counseling. Often this is self-evident, made immediately clear by the first expression of the parishioner. At other times parishioners will report a wide range of concerns in the first session and will have to be asked what should constitute the primary problem focus. The identification of the primary problem focus leads naturally to a formulation of goals for the counseling. These goals will sometimes be quite specific (i.e., to be able to make an informed decision about a potential job change) but will also at times be rather broad (i.e., to be able to express feelings related to an illness). As is illustrated in these examples, some goals will describe an end-point while others will describe more of a process. Maintaining this flexibility in how goals are understood is crucial if Strategic Pastoral Counseling is to be a helpful counseling approach for the broad range of situations faced by the pastoral counselor.

The Engagement Stage

The second stage of Strategic Pastoral Counseling involves the further engagement of the pastor and the one seeking help around the problems and concerns that brought them together. This is the heart of the counseling process. The major tasks of this stage are the exploration of the person's feelings, thoughts, and behavioral patterns associated with the central concerns and the development of new perspectives and strategies for coping or change.

It is important to note that the work of this stage may well begin in the first session. The model should not be interpreted in a rigid or mechanical manner. If the goals of the first stage are completed with time remaining in the first session, one can very appropriately begin to move into the tasks of this next stage. However, once the tasks of Stage 1 are completed, those associated with this second stage become the central focus. If the full five sessions of Strategic Pastoral Counseling are employed, this second stage normally provides the structure for sessions 2, 3, and 4.

The central foci for the three sessions normally associated with this stage are the feelings, thoughts, and behaviors associated with the problem presented by the person seeking help. Although these are usually intertwined, a selective focus on each, one at a time, ensures that each is adequately addressed and that all the crucial dynamics of the person's psychospiritual functioning are considered.

The reason for beginning with feelings is that this is where most people themselves begin when they come to a counselor. But this does not mean that most people know their feelings. The exploration of feelings involves encouraging people to face and express whatever it is that they are feeling, to the end that these feelings can be known and then dealt with appropriately. The goal at this point is to listen and respond empathically to the feelings of those seeking help, not to try to change them.

After an exploration of the major feelings being experienced by the person seeking help, the next task is an exploration of the thoughts associated with these feelings and the development of alternative ways of understanding present experiences. It is in this phase of Strategic Pastoral Counseling that the explicit use of Scripture is usually most appropriate. Bearing in mind the potential misuses and problems that can be associated with such use of religious resources, the pastoral counselor should be, nonetheless, open to a direct presentation of scriptural truths when they offer the possibility of a new and helpful perspective on one's situation.

The final task of the engagement stage of Strategic Pastoral Counseling grows directly out of this work on understanding and involves the exploration of the behavioral components of the person's functioning. Here the pastor explores what concrete things the person is doing in the face of the problems or distressing situations being encountered and together with the parishioner begins to identify changes in behavior that may be desirable. The goal of this stage is to identify changes that both pastor and parishioner agree are important and to begin to establish concrete strategies for making these changes.

The Disengagement Stage

The last session or two involves preparation for the termination of counseling and includes two specific tasks: the evaluation of progress and assessment of remaining concerns, and making arrangements regarding a referral if this is needed.

The evaluation of progress is usually a process that both pastor and parishioner will find rewarding. Some of this may be done during previous sessions. Even when this is the case, it is a good idea to use the last session to undertake a brief review of what has been learned from the counseling. Closely associated with this, of course, is an identification of remaining concerns. Seldom is everything resolved after five sessions. This means that the parishioner is preparing to leave counseling with some work yet to be done. But he or she does so with plans for the future and the development of these is an important task of the disengagement stage of Strategic Pastoral Counseling.

If significant problems remain at this point, the last couple of sessions should also be used to make referral arrangements. Ideally these should be discussed in the second or third session and they should by now be all arranged. It might even be ideal if by this point the parishioner could have had a first session with the new counselor, thus allowing a processing of this first experience as part of the final pastoral counseling session.

Recognition of one's own limitations of time, experience, training, and ability is an indispensable component of the practice of all professionals. Pastors are no exception. Pastors offering Strategic Pastoral Counseling need, therefore, to be aware of the resources within their community and be prepared to refer parishioners for help that they can better receive elsewhere.

In the vast majority of cases, the actual termination of a Strategic Pastoral Counseling relationship goes very smoothly. Most often both pastor and parishioner agree that there is no further need to meet and they find easy agreement with, even if some sadness around, the decision to discontinue the counseling sessions. However, there may be times when this process is somewhat difficult. This will sometimes be due to the parishioner's desire to continue to meet. At other times the difficulty in terminating will reside within the pastor. Regardless, the best course of action is usually to follow through on the initial limits agreed upon by both parties.

The exception to this rule is a situation where the parishioner is facing some significant stress or crisis at the end of the five sessions and where there are no other available resources to provide the support needed. If this is the situation, an extension of a few sessions may be appropriate. However, this should again be time-limited and should take the form of crisis management. It should not involve more sessions than is absolutely necessary to restore some degree of stability or to introduce the parishioner to other people who can be of assistance.

Conclusion

Strategic Pastoral Counseling provides a framework for pastors who seek to counsel in a way that is congruent with the rest of their pastoral responsibilities, psychologically informed and responsible. While skill in implementing the model comes only over time, because the approach is focused and time-limited it is quite possible for most pastors to acquire these skills. However, counseling skills cannot be adequately learned simply by reading books. As with all interpersonal skills, they must be learned through practice, and ideally, this practice is best acquired in a context of supervisory feedback from a more experienced pastoral counselor.

The pastor who has mastered the skills of Strategic Pastoral Counseling is in a position to proclaim the Word of God in a highly personalized and relevant manner to people who are often desperate for help. This is a unique and richly rewarding opportunity. Rather than scattering seed in a broadcast manner across ground that is often stony and hard even if at places it is also fertile and receptive to growth, the pastoral counselor has the opportunity to carefully plant one seed at a time. Knowing the soil conditions, he or she is also able to plant it in a highly individualized manner, taking pains to ensure that it will not be quickly blown away, and then gently watering and nourishing its growth. This is the unique opportunity for the ministry of Strategic Pastoral Counseling. It is my prayer that pastors will see the centrality of counseling to their call to ministry, feel encouraged by the presence of an approach to pastoral counseling that lies within their skills and time availability, and will take up these responsibilities with renewed vigor and clarity of direction.

1

Defining Guilt and Shame

I sometimes think that shame, mere awkward, senseless shame, does as much towards preventing good acts and straightforward happiness as any of our vices can do.
—C. S. Lewis, *A Grief Observed*

The Issues

The two of them sat listening to the sermon, as they often did, speculating about what the other was hearing. For her, one more challenging message meant one more experience of pangs of conscience, even an immobilizing sense of worthlessness and shame. She was only vaguely aware of her feelings, however, because she quickly became numb and cold inside. Her husband, on the other hand, listening to the same words, was at complete ease, even feeling a little self-righteous. He always felt confident sitting in church, and the pastor's words of warning about self-centeredness and lovelessness were surely aimed at the guy in the next pew. He wondered whether her stony look meant that she was taking the world's sin on her shoulders—a reaction that always mystified him—while

27

she risked a thought that maybe, just maybe, he would take *this* message to heart.

As the pastor prepared his thoughts for the appointment the woman had made with him the following week, he speculated that again the issue would probably be how to soothe her troubled conscience, and how to put a dent in her husband's. He recalled the old aphorism about the pastoral role—to comfort the afflicted and to afflict the comfortable. The more he thought about it, however, the more he realized how many unanswered questions still lingered in his own mind. *How can one person's conscience be so fragile, and that of another be so resilient? When should a Christian have a sense of guilt, and when should a believer claim freedom from guilt's blemish? How can you inspire a godly repentance, or exculpate the penitent soul? What can be done for a person who is so easily unsettled, and is so often manipulated by others who prey on a sensitive heart? For that matter,* thought the pastor, *how do I sort out my own vacillating feelings of doubt and inadequacy in the pastoral role? How do I respond to the pressures of expectations and preferences in the congregation? When can I say before God that I did what he wanted me to do—nothing more and nothing less?*

The Christian gospel has always said that the universal spiritual crisis in the human race is guilt and shame. Ever since Eden we have had to struggle with a fallen nature that constantly gets us into trouble. We know that in thought, word, and deed, we fall short. The residual feeling that has resulted is, at its strongest, a sense of regret or remorse, but can be a more subtle embarrassment or shyness. In a word, we are left with shame.

The shame that results from our own guilt or that of others is a very complex and evasive experience. On the one hand, if we stop and think about it, we can all recognize plenty of times when we blush, or avoid eye contact with someone, or feel like crawling into a hole. Shame is a universal experience. On the other hand, our reactions vary considerably. One person may believe he is no more than a worm, and another will behave so narcissistically that he will act as if he is his own god, never caring whose rules he breaks or rights he steps on. Yet even in the seemingly shameless personality, there often lurks a deep, dark self-loathing that is so horrifying to face that the conscience is simply walled off.

Of course, these are not new issues in counseling. Recently, however, these themes have become a new focus of discussion in the psychological community. Ever widening circles of people are finding and devouring books and tapes aimed at helping them through their struggles with guilt and shame. In the background is a maturing professional literature. Its writers are using the concepts of shame and guilt as a fundamental new construct and a tool to evaluate and modify some of the classical theories of personality.

The importance for pastoral care is obvious. The pastor is frequently in the position of being a kind of external conscience to the person seeking counsel. The questions people ask are profoundly important: Are bad things happening to me because I am guilty before God? Why do I feel so distant from God? Why do I feel so guilty when I read the Scriptures that I can barely read them anymore? Then again, pastors are frequently those who have to confront people who are shameless about the hurtful things they are doing to others.

Yet when the pastor has to make moral and spiritual judgments he has to test his perspective so that he does not carelessly deliver uninformed edicts. The moral advice of a pastor carries a great deal of weight in the minds of many people. Pastors should be aware that some people will unconsciously read out of the pastors' words the very voice of the Holy Spirit. Like the tense moment in a courtroom when the audience awaits the verdict read by the jury, so many people will wait to hear whether the pastor will say "guilty" or "not guilty." Indeed, pastors need to carefully consider the process whereby they come to that point in pastoral counseling. Nobody will be helped with quick and easy verdicts from spiritual leaders.

Guilt and shame have long been recognized as central spiritual ideas. Every religion is an expression of what is wrong in the world, and how it might be set right. Those that assume a single, personal deity—Judaism, Christianity, Islam—define the world's problem as the human problem of transgression against divine will. Christian faith in particular is built around the hope of forgiveness and grace, renewal and reformation—all set against the dark backdrop of a universal spiritual flaw in human beings. Guilt is the flaw, and shame its signal. Within various Christian traditions we find differing and nuanced answers to questions like: How deep and wide is this guilt problem? When and how is it solved? How does the experience of shame and its alleviation fit into the progress of salvation?

In chapter after chapter of biblical revelation the themes of guilt and shame appear. In the archetypal story of human experience—that of Adam and Eve—we hear this sound endorsement of their original state: "The man and his wife were both naked, and they felt no shame" (Gen. 2:25). The ideal human state includes no shame, simply because there was no guilt. This important statement from the book of beginnings is about more than clothing. It speaks of a guiltless humanity that has no reason to hide what it has done or what it is. But only the thin line of one commandment, and one transgression of that commandment, separated the shame-free transparency of Adam and Eve from their fig leaves and cowering in the garden. They hid themselves, and they hid from God. The second generation repeats the pattern of the first. Before Cain took the life of his brother he experienced a spiritual crisis of his own. His attitudes produced an unacceptable offering, and he found himself caught in a downward spiral of guilt and shame. God asks Cain, "Why are you angry? Why is your face downcast?" (Gen. 4:6). The characteristic posture of shame, the downcast face, is the shape of human countenance when experiencing real guilt. Sadly, Cain's story is not one of humanity having a second chance at innocence, but rather the heritage of human nature falling short.

In the late twentieth century, sophisticated and scientific though it be, this issue is no less alive. Indeed, it has often been said that guilt and shame are where spirituality and psychology meet. It is virtually impossible to talk about such experiences without raising the question of morality, law, sin, the will of God, and the Judeo-Christian heritage. Pastors need to be clear in their thinking on these principles so that when they respond to those seeking pastoral counsel they will have a framework from which to respond.

Toward Some Definitions

Before we get too far down the road we need to define our terms carefully. The words "shame" and "guilt" are used in everyday speech with varying connotations. Some assume that the distinction is one of intensity—shame as guilt in capital letters. We do not hesitate to say we "feel guilty," especially if it is about something with no great stigma, like eating ice cream or forgetting to send a birthday card. Guilt is a socially acceptable label, and may be the best way to show others you are not arrogant or conceited. It is also a way to describe our passing hesitations and distresses. I might have bought that car, except I would have "felt guilty." I explain that I know I stepped out of line in something I said because now I am "feeling guilty." If I ever get around to describing myself as ashamed, however, you know that I *really* "feel guilty." I have stepped beyond the socially acceptable, and now maybe people will think less of me. In the end, however, there are shortcomings in defining shame as intense guilt or guilt as mild shame.

Another popular approach is to define guilt as a personal reaction of regret following a specific mistake or transgression, whereas shame is an internal judgment against one's very being. One popular author puts it this way: "Guilt says I've done something wrong; shame says there is something wrong with me. Guilt says I've made a mistake; shame says I am a mistake. Guilt says what I did was not good; shame says I am no good" (Bradshaw 1988, p. 2). Guilt is an emotional reaction that can be linked to behavior. Shame is a self-contempt and condemnation by which people devalue and discredit their whole personality. It may be that occasionally we experience shame in a helpful way, call it "healthy shame" perhaps, but more often shame is a toxic, destructive experience that only serves to debilitate us.

With this kind of distinction between guilt and shame some important principles may be forgotten, however. First, we may think of guilt only as an experience. In the historical use of the word, however, guilt is mainly an objective judgment of human actions. Guilt is the *fact* of being in the wrong, whether one recognizes it or not. Its opposite is innocence, which also is an issue of objective status. In a courtroom a judge, a jury, and legal advocates spend a great deal of time and attention trying to determine the guilt or innocence of the defendant. It matters very little what the defendant is feeling during the trial. The only real issue is the legal and moral evaluation of his or her actions as compared with an objective standard—the law. It is indeed not at all surprising that in a relativistic age where we are nervous about categories of right and wrong, that we would speak freely about "feeling guilty" but not about "being guilty." The second problem with these common definitions is that they do not recognize that the subjective experiences that we call regret, remorse, embarrassment, mortification, guilt, shame, are really all of a kind. Thus, it will be helpful to use one umbrella term to encompass them all, the most accurate term being "shame." What ties all these states of the heart together is the sense of pulling back, of withdrawing, of hiding. It might be simple embarrassment at having mistakenly worn two different color socks, or it might be the devastation of feeling rejected by another. As different as these situations are, they produce that common emotional response of feeling exposed, of wanting to hide, of losing face.

In this book we will stress the historical root definitions of these two words. Why? Because when we deal with "guilty" people, we should have a conceptual framework on which we base our counsel that includes a theological and philosophical understanding of guilt and shame, as well as a psychological understanding of these experiences. We need to know what the Bible means by sin and responsibility as well as victimization and accusation. We need to be able to help people know what they are responsible for and what they don't have to worry about. We need to understand the psychological experience of shame. Many books have been written in the past about guilt, and in recent times there has been a steady stream of books and articles focusing on the powerful phenomenon of shame. Rarely, however, do we stop to put the moral, spiritual, and psychological realities into an integrated whole.

There are also compelling practical reasons for preserving the objective concept of guilt. It is important that when a person comes to a pastor feeling overwhelmingly ashamed, the question of whether that person really has something to be ashamed about— whether he or she is guilty—be a central subject of discussion.

Indeed, this perhaps will be the primary question on the pastoral counselor's mind. A woman's mother and sister tell her that she is to blame for the long string of personal tragedies in the family, that if only she hadn't moved out so soon her father wouldn't have gone off the wagon again and her brother wouldn't have committed suicide. The woman feels great shame—but is she guilty? One pastor pays a hospital visit to a rape victim who is paralyzed by shame, and another sees the shame-filled rapist in the county jail. At times like this, we need standards of innocence and guilt so that we can lead the victim to feel the lightness of innocence, and the victimizer the burden of guilt.

The Meaning of Guilt

Only in the latter part of this century has the notion of "feeling guilty" almost entirely supplanted the idea of "being guilty." Were you to ask people on the street to define "guilt" they might very well offer something like, "It's what you feel when you think you've done something wrong." It is the message of the sign at a national frozen yogurt chain: "all of the pleasure, none of the guilt." It is natural that we associate an emotional state with something as significant as the fear of being in the wrong. Our God-given sensitivity to wrong-doing does produce an internal tension or pain. A serious problem arises, however, when our *entire* concept of guilt is an emotional experience. Then we confuse the by-product with the cause.

Yet the forensic meaning of guilt is not entirely lost in our vocabulary and in our thinking ("forensic" means objective or legal). We do know about law courts and their purpose in determining guilt or innocence. If you are a defendant in a trial, you know that there will be one of two outcomes. You will either walk freely out of the court if the judge or jury returns a "not guilty" verdict, or you will fall under the sanctions of the court if pronounced "guilty." The issue is solely whether you violated the standards of an objective rule, the law. So should we evaluate many of our actions on a day-by-day basis. If someone has great emotional distress because he bought stock with inside information, the issue is not just how to deal with the feelings, but how to judge the actions. If a husband is laden with shame because his wife is blaming him for everything that is wrong in their marriage, he needs to sort out where he has been guilty and where not. The teenager who tells his parents not to lay one more "guilt trip" on him needs not just to react to his parents' voices, but to figure out whether there is any truth in their judgment of his actions.

We find in the dictionary the original objective idea of guilt. Webster's defines guilt as "the fact of being responsible for an offense or wrongdoing." Only *secondarily* does it list "remorseful awareness of having done something wrong or of having failed to do something required or expected." The Oxford English Dictionary, the most standard lexicon of the English language, overwhelmingly stresses the forensic definitions: guilt is "a failure of duty, delinquency; offense, crime, sin; responsibility for an action or event; the fact of having committed some specified or implied offense; criminality; culpability."

Guilt begins as a question of status. Am I guilty or not? Is someone else besides me the actual guilty party? Shakespeare's King Lear is familiar with the tactic of applying guilt where it does not belong—of blaming—if no one else, then perhaps the stars: "we make guilty of our own disasters the sun, the moon and the stars; as if we were villains by necessity, fools by heavenly compulsion" (*King Lear* 1.02.120).

Sometimes when we speak of "guilt" we include both the forensic meaning and the emotional response. With an issue as weighty as that of guilt, it should not surprise us that we closely link it with the most commonly associated *emotional* responses. The remorse and regret we feel when we realize we are guilty gets blended into the entire experience—moral judgment and affective response merge—and thus we often speak of our "guilt," meaning both the culpable standing we have because of a misdeed and the feelings of shame that accompany it.

The danger we need to avoid is forgetting entirely the moral, theological, and ethical issues of objective right and wrong as we evaluate our feelings of guilt or shame. The danger is if we view the feelings as the only problem. Perhaps they are the primary problem if such feelings were improperly imposed upon us by others. Then again, we always need to consider that in a given situation, we really may be guilty. To try to resolve our "guilty" feelings without getting at the issue of moral judgment is a plan of action that can be as ineffective as pulling weeds without getting the roots.

Pastors should know that a central part of their role as ministers of the gospel is to hold forth the moral requirements of the law of God. Discovering our moral needs, and moral failures, moves us toward dependence upon God. The law is doing its job as tutor leading us to Christ ("the law was put in charge to lead us to Christ" [Gal. 3:24]). For some pastors, this comes quite easily. Because of temperament or belief, they have no problem telling other people their faults. The potential danger, of course, is that such a pastor might in an undiscerning way blast away at the consciences of people believing all along that he or she is carrying out the normal function of pastoral care.

There is law (which shows us our need), and gospel (which shows God's supply of grace). Some pastors are naturally inclined toward a proclamation of gospel. While this is certainly a biblical view of pastoral care, pastors need to make sure that they do not avoid looking at the hard realities of guilt in those they counsel. It is not easy to talk about guilt. Pastors should know themselves well enough so that, if they are by temperament inclined to avoid the issue of guilt, they can properly adjust their responses to others.

We should not be surprised that these moral issues have not by and large been the concern of secular psychology. First, psychiatrists and psychologists do not see moral judgments as central to the domain of their disciplines. This may be by professional principle, a kind of boundary-setting that allows for empathy and acceptance in the therapeutic process, or it may arise out of a modern skepticism about systems of morality in general. If one believes that morality and ethics are entirely variable and relative, then of course there will be great hesitation in bringing categories of right and wrong into the therapeutic process. If a married man presents himself as a habitual womanizer, the secular therapist may hesitate to bring into the discussion such morally charged words as adultery, infidelity, unfaithfulness, and objective guilt.

Yet when people come to their pastors with issues of guilt and shame in their lives, they are often seeking a real cleansing. They know that there are real moral issues in life. Any solution applied that seeks to simply evacuate moral categories from a person's life will in the end be short-lived.

Another dynamic that turns us away from acceptance of guilt is the fear of facing a problem for which there is no solution at hand. Who wants to accept a sentence of "guilty" if there is no hope for pardon or parole? Here is where the distinct strength of pastoral counseling comes in. The pastoral counselor can bravely consider the possibility of real guilt because of a belief that there is, in Christ, a solution at hand. Forgiveness is at the core of the gospel; it is what God wants to do; it is what people are supposed to do for each other. In the modern world the secularist may cower at the question of real guilt because with no assurance of a treatment, it is hard to accept the sobering diagnosis of "guilty."

The concept of guilt should actually be a comfort to us. In the world of law, we are protected from the wrongdoing of others (and are guided into civilized life) because there is law, and a pronouncement of "guilty" on those who violate its standards. Any civilized society is a society of law. The same principles apply to morality—the personal kind of law that has transcendent meaning. There are rights and wrongs in life, and that means that sometimes we will be in the right and protected from the wrongs of others; but if we are in the wrong, we need to own up to our guilt. To separate ourselves from these convictions is to set ourselves adrift from the moorings that have historically held Western civilization together.

Of course, all this does not mean that the role of the pastoral counselor is to probe around for guilt in the person being counseled until he or she finds it. But neither will it do to automatically absolve the person being counseled of all guilt by assuming that someone else is to blame. One of the greatest challenges for any counselor is carefully to discern the subtleties of a situation in order to be able to carefully and cautiously assign responsibility where it is due. *The pastoral counselor is much more than a judge, but not less than a judge.* The pastoral counselor is the dispenser of care and concern, of empathy and compassion, but at the same time must use discernment and objectivity to help the person being counseled to come to understand where blame is to be laid.

It would make it all very easy if shame were the predictable signal of guilt, but it often does not work that way. Take the case of

Jim and Janice. Jim has been drinking heavily for years, and, not surprisingly, their family is a mess. Jim does not own his guilt but instead blames Janice for her lack of care for him. Janice believes it, and is bound by a daily shame that only increases the worse Jim's behavior. She assumes the guilt and experiences the shame while Jim ignores his guilt and behaves shamelessly. They are both under the illusion that their children are unaffected, but the rancorous atmosphere of the home has only ensured for the children a sense of shame about themselves and an inner questioning: What did I do to make Daddy act that way? How did I make Mom so sad? What can I do to fix my family? These disaster stories sometimes do have a happy ending. How thrilling it is to see a family where guilt is properly confessed and the healing of shame begins. But there is no shortcut around guilt and shame.

The Experience of Shame

There is a common thread that runs through that whole range of experiences so familiar to us which we may variously call embarrassment, humiliation, disgrace, guilt, shame, low self-esteem, self-deprecation. As different as these terms sound, they represent merely the difference of intensity and form of a single *type* of affective (emotional) experience. Psychologists group affective experiences together based upon common symptoms. The tie between simple embarrassment and self-denigration is a sense of cowering, or hiding, or withdrawal. You might say, "I feel like crawling into a hole," or something similar, and by it you mean that something has happened to trigger in you a negative feeling toward yourself that says you are unworthy, that you should conceal yourself. It might be that you hurt someone, and you feel ashamed. Or for another person with an entirely different experience it may be receiving a promotion or an award, and, amazing as it seems, this good turn of fortune produces a sense of shame. Self-doubts linger in the shadows, waiting for any signal—good or bad—to jump out and criticize.

"Shame" is perhaps the best label for describing this range of experiences. It has become somewhat popular to use "guilt" to describe the negative feelings arising after an act of wrongdoing and "shame" for the general negative view of self that afflicts many people. But for three main reasons, in this book we will use "shame" as the overarching term for the affective experience, and "guilt" in its primary sense of the fact of wrongdoing—not as a label for a feeling at all, but as the objective status of being in the wrong.

First, we need to recognize the demonstrable links between the various forms and intensities of shame. By understanding these links we will better recognize shame when we experience it, and we will more effectively and appropriately deal with it. Gershen Kaufman, a leading writer on the subject of shame, says, "Having so many different names for its various manifestations has hindered recognition of the underlying affect of shame." Though discouragement, embarrassment, shyness, or shame may be experienced differently "yet their core effect is identical" (Kaufman 1989, 22). A second reason for using "guilt" for the objective and "shame" for the subjective is that there is a threat to our moral sensitivity if we forget the primary meaning of guilt as a forensic fact. And finally, we should be leery of distinctions that attempt to separate actions from self, which is commonly encountered in many modern discussions of shame. Contrary to what is sometimes said about guilt and shame, there is no clear boundary between what we feel about what we do and about who we are. Kaufman points out that this traditional way of differentiating guilt and shame is misleading: "The assumption that we feel guilty about deeds but feel shame about self is equally in error. The target of shame can be either the self or the self's actions. . . . From the perspective of affect theory, one can feel shameful about deeds as well as guilty about self." A person may experience shame as a general view of self, but the same kind of emotion is experienced when there is remorse connected to actions.

The sources and occasions for shame may vary greatly from one person to another. Some people feel shame mostly when they do something wrong. Others experience the same *kind* of feelings in circumstances in which they are in no way guilty (see Tables 1.1 and 1.2). They are people who take blame on themselves, who feel ashamed when they have another emotion like fear, anger, or even joy. What can be agreed upon is that shame is a problem; nobody wants to experience it. We may feel shame because we are guilty, or when we are not guilty at all. But we will properly deal with it only if we ask ourselves if it is the by-product of guilt. In the midst of his terrible dilemma, Job asked himself just this question: "If I am guilty—woe to me! Even if I am innocent, I cannot lift my head, for I am full of shame and drowned in my affliction" (10:15). Job's shame was not the result of being guilty. That was the rash judgment of his "counselors," who worked a peculiar logic backwards: Job is physically afflicted; thus he must be guilty of some grave sin against God. All Job knew is that in his disheartened state he felt like shrinking back. He says he could not raise his head, that characteristic feeling of wanting to cast our eyes downward when we feel ashamed. He wondered whether he was guilty, though he thought not. Job needed some time to understand guilt and shame. How different the sentiment of Shakespeare's Juliet who says of her Romeo: "he was not born to shame; Upon his brow shame is asham'd to sit" (*Romeo and Juliet* 3.02.92). Though Romeo had just killed a man in a fight, Juliet's judgment (biased, admittedly) is that he was entirely clean of guilt and shame.

Psychologists describe the common symptoms of the shame experience. According to Silvan Tomkins:

> Shame is the affect of indignity, of defeat, of transgression and of alienation. . . . Shame is felt as an inner torment, a sickness of the soul. It does not matter whether the humiliated one has been shamed by derisive laughter or whether he mocks himself. In either event he feels himself naked, defeated, alienated, lacking in dignity or worth. (Tomkins 1963, 118)

We could say that shame is written all over a person's face. What do we do when we are ashamed? We turn our eyes downward, avoiding eye contact as a part of withdrawal or hiding. We might even hang our heads. And, most telling of all, is the conspicuous blush. The fair-skinned, really talented blushers of this world have this facial readout that tells everyone around them, "I'm ashamed right now!" Blushing is not usually a characteristic desired by the blusher, but, when we think of it, don't we like a blusher all the more for his or her blushing? Any honest person will think, *Even though my face doesn't show it, I often feel the same way that person looks.* Such are the simple physical symptoms that psychological researchers have documented in this category of experience we call shame.

The pastoral counselor needs to have wide-opened eyes. The counselee may give conspicuous nonverbal clues of serious issues of shame. Does he or she have very poor eye contact? Is there a stooped posture? Does he or she sit back and away from you? Is there a moment in the discussion when his or her head is hanging? Does the person look dull and lifeless? Is there blushing, and when? Such are the telltale signs of the experience of shame.

There are also well documented patterns of how we defend ourselves against the pain of feeling shame. To "save face" as we say, we may have developed the habit of pulling our heads backwards rigidly, trying to look unabashed. That is why our parents told us to "keep our chin up." No one wants to suffer the indignity of "losing face." Under other circumstances we may paste on a look of contempt, or just freeze the face in an emotionless mask. To let others know that we feel ashamed will only add shame on top of shame. Some hide behind performance instead. If the ego is threatened with shame, the person goes to work, doing that function or profession or bearing that role that has always scored points with others. Here is the doctor or pastor or helpful neighbor who has little joy in service, because the performance is a desperate move to cover over shame.

Shame can be a very powerful emotion and, as such, it can have a binding effect on some people. A cloud of emotional pain comes over them, and they are almost paralyzed by the sense of disgrace or exposure. They may abruptly drop out of conversations, or they may cut off relationships that produce too much shame. They sometimes avoid contact with other people. Interacting in a group setting may seem to be harder than facing death. And they feel bound in their relationship with God. Either God is too threatening or too elusive or too unpredictable to be trusted. Others, wanting so desperately to feel close to God, take the lunge of faith toward him, but are bewildered when they still feel unsettled and disconnected. Shame is getting in the way.

Table 1.1
Characteristics of the Shame Experience:
Healthy Dimensions

- sense of humility and need for God
- embarrassment about breaking social norms
- realistic understanding of personal imperfections
- responsiveness to internalized morals and values

Table 1.2
Characteristics of the Shame Experience:
Unhealthy Dimensions

- fear of vulnerability and exposure of self; a sense of waiting to be found out
- feeling like an outsider, disconnected, lonely
- defensiveness
- perfectionism
- fear of intimacy and commitments
- impairment of friendships; looking to "rescue" others
- getting stuck in dependent or counterdependent relationships
- shyness, feelings of inferiority or worthlessness often resulting in social withdrawal
- anger, jealousy, and judgmental attitudes toward others
- difficulty in accepting forgiveness
- feeling distant from God
- legalistic ways of thinking
- use of compulsive behaviors to block painful feelings
- use of excuses, rationalizations, lies
- blaming others
- self-centeredness or selfishness
- exaggerated sense of personal flaws or ugliness
- sense of powerlessness and inability to change
- depression and even suicidal tendencies

The pastor was shocked to hear the story of one of his deacons. A man who was well known in the church and had held many positions of responsibility was now telling him that he could not remember when he last felt close to God or a genuine desire to draw close to him. He had been going through the motions for years. But he had always felt that he was chasing after something, or perhaps it was that he was running from something. He said that if anybody in the church really knew what kind of person he was, they wouldn't want to have anything to do with him. He was now wondering whether his dogmatic stances and need to be in authority were his tactics for dealing with his fear of exposure. It had all come to a head now because he was feeling old enough to feel tired of trying, lonely enough to question whether he was really in fellowship, sad enough not to care if he looked humiliated, and desperate enough to lower his guard and confide in a spiritual leader. The pastor had his work cut out for him. Did the shame begin with a hidden guilt from the distant past, or was the shame simply mud smeared on the windows of the man's life so that no light was getting in? Either might be possible, and each would require a different solution.

This is the kind of situation that Strategic Pastoral Counseling in the context of the church should aim at preventing. Where the fruit of the Spirit—love, joy, peace, patience, kindness, goodness, faithfulness, gentleness, self-control—is lacking, the Christian misses the unique opportunity to enjoy the graces of Christ and be an effective witness for him. Shame, if not dealt with properly, can choke out what should be the developing life of a tree planted by streams of living water.

A Comprehensive Model of Guilt and Shame

The pastor will be best equipped to deal with the issues of guilt and shame when he or she has in mind a comprehensive theory that accounts for and coordinates the many elements contributed by a biblical theology and sound psychological study. What will such an inclusive theory of guilt and shame have to accomplish? It will have to be responsive to many realities that we know from biblical revelation: (1) the human race is universally guilty; (2) this state of guilt has influenced every natural human ability—moral, spiritual, intellectual, emotional, relational; (3) God has provided the means for reforming the person and cleansing the conscience; (4) false accusation and falsely perceived guilt cause confusion.

An inclusive theory of guilt and shame should also incorporate the realities that we know from psychological study: (1) shame is a universal human reaction appearing early in development; (2) shame can be an appropriate reaction to correction or chastisement; (3) shame can also be the response of someone who is being manipulated and controlled by others; and (4) shame includes a wide range of manifestations from the experience of simple shyness or embarrassment to crippling self-depreciation.

The model that will form the foundation of this book will point to guilt in its primary sense: the fact of having violated a moral, legal, or social norm. Shame is that whole range of subjective experiences, the emotions, that are commonly described as embarrassment, regret, remorse, feeling guilty, feeling worthless. To account for the widely different experiences of shame our basic paradigm will be a three fold model of shame that includes moral shame, imposed shame, and natural shame (see Table 1.3).

Table 1.3
Brief Definitions

guilt	the fact of wrongdoing, being in the wrong
moral shame	regret or remorse for having done wrong
imposed shame	disgrace or devaluation inflicted by another
natural shame	a sense of limitation, fallibility, humility

Moral Shame

Moral shame is that regret or remorse that is a response to some specific failure in a particular act or habit. Moral shame is the result of simple moral sensitivity or conscience. It is the way God made us. As the sense of touch is the sensitivity that protects us from physical harm, the flash of moral shame in a person's conscience when that person fails in a commitment or takes something that is not his or hers, or hurts someone through carelessness, is an uncomfortable but necessary affective experience. It may be slight and passing for a minor offense, or a major wound in the case of a great transgression. To complicate matters, however, because the conscience is not failproof in itself, one might have extreme moral shame for a minor offense, or only a hint of shame for a real crime. The shame response needs constant training. God's solution for moral shame is simple forgiveness. We quote 1 John 1:9 as often as we do because we know how common is our transgression and our desire for reconciliation: "if we confess our sins, he is faithful and just and will forgive us our sins and purify us from all unrighteousness." The previous verse (a little less-often quoted) highlights the necessity for moral shame: "if we claim to be without sin, we deceive ourselves and the truth is not in us."

Imposed Shame

Imposed shame is that sense of personal disgrace or worthlessness that has resulted from the words or actions of others. The cause may be belittling, neglect, abandonment, or any other action that devalues another. Imposed shame can be an occasional experience, as when someone tries to influence another by manipulating his or her conscience. All too often the long-term shaming that defenseless children are subjected to results in a shaping of their whole personalities. Such people in their adult lives may need major emotional healing to be able to sense the genuine love of God or others. In marriages the crowbar of imposed shame is often the tool of choice for one partner to manipulate the other into a state of subjection. The motive behind imposed shame is often that of control, which is why the Bible calls Satan the Accuser, the one whose strategy is control through spiritual crippling. If you can make someone feel low, you can tower over him. The solution to imposed shame is a reattribution of guilt. If someone tries to make me feel ashamed for something I know I am not responsible for, I must turn the tables and at least in my own mind assert that it is the imposer who is in the wrong, not I. The Christian knows that because God is the Lord of justice and truth, he will always endorse the proper placing of blame.

Natural Shame

When we have accounted for moral shame (the twist of conscience that occurs when we fail), and then imposed shame (that kind of shame that is inflicted by others), there still remains in our experience a type of shame that is in the background—a general sense that we as human beings have limitations and a nature that is given to mistakes. Natural shame is that general sense that most people have that they are incomplete creatures who live in an incomplete world. This is what Christians mean by "fallenness," and what they accept as a biblical view of life. We do fall short; we are fallible and frail and limited. It was not our created nature, but it is what human nature has become. The unnatural has become natural. The person with an appropriate grasp of natural shame will say, "I will try my best today, but I will not live a perfect life. I accept the fact that I will have to apologize to people and to God throughout my life, because I know I will never be perfect in this life. If I hide from my natural shame I will only set myself and others up for disaster because I'll not be living in reality." There is, then, a general sense of humility that human beings must accept. Yet God offers a treatment for guilt in this life. When by the grace of God we receive the justification and redemption that is found in Christ, we are accepted into the eternal family of God. We are forgiven our sins, past, present, and future, and God begins to reshape the human form he originally created. We enjoy a treatment but not a total cure for sin in this life, and so the necessity for the humbling effects of natural shame.

The pastoral counselor is in a unique position to be able to help those troubled with guilt and shame because there is a way to address all the moral and emotional issues that neither sacrifices moral categories nor denies real psychological distress. This is all the more important today because the solutions offered often ignore the reality of damaged souls ("the only problem people have is their unconfessed sin"), or the importance of moral responsibility ("shame is the problem, not guilt").

Furthermore, in a most wonderful way, the Christian gospel has always been a comprehensive solution—the only comprehensive solution—to all our problems with guilt and shame. Insofar as the crucified Savior provides forgiveness and justification, any human being can have, by faith, a total solution for guilt. Thereafter the sting of moral shame can be lessened, and when the believer does sin and experiences the stab of moral shame, he or she can confess and realize anew God's great forgiveness. The Christian gospel addresses imposed shame in that God constantly depicts himself as the vindicator of the falsely accused, and even took upon himself the position of the accused on the cross. Finally, for natural shame God provides the assurance that he accepts us as fallen creatures, and that he will work with us in a process that will improve us, while never putting us in the position of having to be perfect to warrant his love.

2

Shame in Three Forms

A father returned home from a long day at work tired and distracted. He was greeted exuberantly by his daughter; he wanted to ask his wife a question but she was not in sight; and the cats were fighting underfoot. Amidst this confusion, he noticed his one-year-old son standing with outstretched arms and on tiptoes, reaching toward his father. A moment later, he again glanced down and noticed the boy no longer held his arms upward. The boy, who had only moments earlier asked to be held by his father, now stood very still, arms at his side and glancing toward the floor. The boy had longed to connect with his father and when this did not occur, the son felt shame.

A sixteen-year-old son was given permission to use the family car on a Friday night. When the son returned home two hours past his curfew, he attempted to sneak in through the back door. Nearing his bedroom, he was met by his father who merely said, "I'm glad you're home. We'll talk in the morning." The son froze, sensed a great heaviness, and looked down, feeling great shame.

For both of these sons, the emotion of shame dominated their experience. The young boy was not guilty of a transgression; the teenage boy clearly was. While their emotional experiences were

47

similar, the means of resolving these situations were quite different. The young boy's shame was released when the father touched him and then held him. Instantly, life and energy returned as he hugged his father. The teenage boy was held accountable for his wrongdoing and his shame was released when the father extended forgiveness.

In a very different situation, a woman experienced a painful gnawing at her soul as she looked at her plans for the day. Even with her best efforts, she realized that she would fall short of meeting all the demands before her. As she reflected on this, she sensed that she was not adequate, that something was missing. She had done nothing wrong and no one else was involved. In this private moment, it seemed that things were not the way they were supposed to be.

The emotion of shame occurs when people experience a disconnection between themselves and other people or God, or within themselves. It is a feeling of separation, detachment, or even alienation. The young boy wanted to be connected emotionally and physically with his father and allowed himself to be vulnerable in expressing his desire for connection. When the father did not connect with the son, the son's automatic reaction was to protect himself from the pain of the disconnection. Shame functions to alarm us to the state of disconnection and to protect us from the consequences of disconnection from another.

While the experiences felt similar, the causes were different. We feel the emotion of shame at times of perceived disconnection, no matter what the cause. In this chapter, an original threefold model of shame will be presented that outlines the various forms and causes of shame and identifies the processes for shame resolution. Congruent with the psychological research in Tomkins' (1962, 1963) and Kaufman's (1989) reformulation, this model strives to provide an integration of theological truths and psychological findings.

It is important for the pastoral counselor to have a conceptual understanding of guilt and shame. An understanding of the causes of the shame experience can facilitate empathy and understanding for those caught in shame's grasp. The pastor can provide an understanding to the counselee that often facilitates hope. In addition, an understanding of the causes of shame and the difference between shame and guilt provides a means for the resolution of shame and guilt. The pastor's focus during a counseling session—the questions asked, observations noted, and conclusions drawn—is greatly influenced by the pastor's understanding of the problem. In addition, the pastor can use this conceptual model to help the counselee understand the integration of our spiritual and psychological selves. An understanding of the cause of shame leads to understanding the process of shame resolution.

Shame is resolved with reconnection. The young boy was free of shame once his father touched him, and the teenager experienced release from the shame following his father's forgiveness.

The common thread between guilt and shame may be understood in the dynamics of being connected, disconnected, and reconnected. Human beings desire and have an inborn need to be connected. The experience of disconnection is painful. "Connection" involves a meeting of the hearts, an openness and vulnerability, a giving and receiving, a recognition and responsiveness to the other person, and communication that the person is valuable. Connection includes being touched, heard, or seen. The emotions are involved when two people connect, for we only connect at points of vulnerability.

From the beginning people were created to have fellowship with God and one another. The deep and intimate connection in the garden before the fall is evident in the description of Adam and Eve as "naked" and without shame (Gen. 2:25). Upon the transgression, Adam and Eve experienced disconnection and displayed common reactions to shame, hiding and blaming others. Their choice to disobey resulted in the first disconnection from God. The effects of sin have been the disconnection between people, between God and people, between people and themselves, and between people and their environment (Gen. 3:14–19). All human attempts to reconnect have been futile. As a small boy cannot make his father connect with him, it is only through the heavenly Father's reaching out to his children that reconnection may occur and shame be released.

Shame is felt by the person who experiences the disconnection. Not only does the emotional pain of the shame alarm the person to the disconnection, it also serves to inhibit the person from remaining vulnerable since continued vulnerability will only magnify the disconnection. The person who inadvertently says the wrong thing in a social setting, the young child who misbehaves and disappoints his parents, and the individual who is confronted by colleagues about inadequate performance share a common experience. The pain of the shame serves to inhibit them from further inappropriate acts and thus protects them from further harm. Our limitations and inadequacies are brought to our attention, which can ultimately lead to increased acceptance of who we really are and a reliance on the grace of God.

Thoughts, feelings, needs, wants, and events that occur during a shame experience are "paired," or "bound," with the emotion of shame. If these pairings occur frequently or if the emotional intensity of the shame is high, a repeated instance of the thought, need, want, or event will elicit the feeling of shame and the corresponding sense of disconnection, pain, and inhibition. In other words, an association or link forms in the mind. Shame is triggered sometimes quite unexpectedly—not unlike being transported back in time when you catch a familiar smell from some past moment. If the father of a one-year-old boy does not reconnect with the son as a typical pattern, it is likely that the boy will develop an interpersonal need-shame bind, or a strong pairing between his need for a father, his need for others, his emotional reactions, and the emotion of shame. As a young man, he may feel embarrassed to express his emotional wants or reactions, feel uncomfortable touching other men, or appear to be highly self-sufficient, not needing anyone. Likewise, an overly busy or nonresponsive parent may inadvertently not respond to the connection needs of a child, contributing to an interpersonal need-shame bind with an inhibition or even denial of social needs. Children who meet with criticism regarding their efforts on homework, achievement, or household chores may develop a shame-competence bind in which they feel shame at school or work, or during other activities involving achievement. Being told that "big boys don't cry" may contribute to an affect-shame bind in which shame is triggered at times of emotional response, resulting in an inhibition of feelings. Basic drives of hunger and sexuality may also be paired with shame. The capacity for shame to bind with any aspect of life illustrates the primary role this emotion plays in regulating our behavior and experience.

The person who experiences shame may or may not be responsible for the disconnection, that is, may or may not be guilty. The emotional experience, the feeling of shame, is not sufficient to establish guilt. It is the identification of responsibility for the disconnection that identifies the type of shame that is being experienced. Here shame and guilt intersect. It is only by attaching the shame to the party who is responsible for the disconnection that the shame may be resolved. The pastoral counselor is challenged with the task of helping to discern who is responsible for the disconnection before resolution of the guilt and shame may occur. The reality of guilt and the emotion of shame cannot and should not be ignored; both demand resolution and release from their consequences.

Moral Shame

We experience moral shame, the feelings of remorse or regret for having done something wrong, when we are responsible for the disconnection, when we are guilty. *The disconnection, be it from another person, God, or even the self, is due to actions for which we are responsible.* The identification of moral shame is independent of the person's awareness of his or her responsibility and is dependent upon an objective assessment of the situation. As such, the recognition of moral shame assumes objective standards of right and wrong as well as personal responsibility. At times we need someone to identify for us our personal responsibility, our guilt, while at other times our consciences convict us. The emotional experience is sufficient to identify the presence of the emotion of shame yet insufficient to clarify the type of shame.

Moral shame is an invaluable characteristic of human beings that allows them to live with others, for it is our moral shame that provides the checks and balance between respecting ourselves and respecting others. The fulfillment of the second half of the great commandment, to love our neighbors as ourselves, requires a healthy dose of moral shame. Without it, impulses would govern our lives. Each person would do as he or she pleases, and we would

live in a state of anarchy. The root selfishness and self-centeredness, our sin nature, would be unleashed to its own ends.

A two-year-old may find it enjoyable to hit or bite others and may
seem puzzled when others find this behavior unacceptable. Should
this young child carry these habits into adulthood, he or she would
likely be labeled antisocial and incur the wrath and judgment of
those he or she hurts. What is needed in the young child is some
type of internal regulation that can be paired with the unacceptable behavior of hitting and biting. When people acquire this internal regulation, they may then live peacefully with others. It is
through the disconnection from the parents paired with a specific
behavior and the subsequent reconnection that we learn a moral
code, our conscience is shaped, and we are able to judge right from
wrong. The emotion of shame, with its inhibitory characteristics,
provides the mechanism for this internal regulation.

The Development of Moral Shame

The experience of moral shame can have a positive outcome. An
understanding of the development of moral shame can help the
pastor appreciate the value of this shame experience and to
empathize with those who have had negative or destructive developmental experiences.

The interactions between child and parent are the template for
the child's acquisition of shame. The connection, disconnection,
and reconnection experienced by the child from the parents are
the mechanisms by which shame and an understanding of guilt are
acquired and resolved. The experience of moral shame is the fundamental factor in a person's learning of right and wrong, being
able to socially relate to others and to set personal boundaries.

The discipline of children involves the parents associating some
form of disconnection (a verbal correction, a look, a time-out, a
spanking, etc.) with a behavior, thus establishing a shame-behav-
ior bind, and then reconnecting with the child (a hug, word of forgiveness, etc.), thereby allowing the child to release the shame.
After repeated pairings, the child learns to associate the behavior
with the painful feeling of shame and therefore avoids the behavior in order to avoid the shame and stay connected with the par-

ents. The child has now internalized the values of the parents and will act in a manner that is likely to increase the likelihood he or she can connect with the parents and to decrease the likelihood of the painful feeling of shame. The child has acquired the capacity to experience moral shame as a disconnection from his or her internal representation of the parents.

As children continue to develop, they accept these values as their own—no longer merely as their parents' but as their personal code of ethics. At this point, to violate or act against this code causes a disconnection within themselves, for they have wronged themselves, God, and possibly others.

In adult life we may become aware in many ways that the shame we experience is in fact moral shame. First, our consciences may convict us. However, the conscience is not sufficient since we all use defense mechanisms such as denial or suppression to protect ourselves from the painful awareness of unacceptable realities. Thus, at times other people will bring to our awareness the truth of our guilt. At this moment, the shame felt may seem like imposed shame as another person is involved and we often feel embarrassed when our wrongdoing or inadequacies are exposed. The shame experience, however, is best understood as moral shame because the disconnection between the two people is a result of the wrongdoing by the person experiencing the shame.

Finally, we may become aware of moral shame through the Holy Spirit. God may impact us through our consciences, bringing to our awareness the reality of sin in our lives. God may also use our interpersonal relationships to identify our personal responsibility for wrongdoing and thus expose moral shame. As Nathan came to David and exposed the king's hidden transgressions (2 Sam. 12), so another person may bring to light our unknown or hidden guilt and the corresponding moral shame.

Determining Who Is Responsible

The determination of guilt requires that a standard greater than one's self be used to determine who is responsible for the disconnection. Often the pastor is asked, either directly or by implication, to assist in discerning who is responsible for an offense. The relativism of our society and popular moral codes have been of little help as we struggle to determine who is right and who is wrong, who has been victimized and who is the perpetrator, who is responsible and who is not. Christians have the written Word of God, the work of the Holy Spirit within them, and the fellowship of believers to guide them in this decision-making process.

The rules for determining responsibility for an action flow from our capacity for reason and logic. A person is judged to be responsible for a wrongdoing or harm if his or her behavior caused the wrong. That is, there is a direct causal relationship between something done by a person and the wrongful , harmful, or sinful act. A person's behavior is a cause of wrong or hurt if and only if the harm would not have occurred without the behavior.

Determining moral responsibility requires further analysis. Not all harmful acts or forms of disconnection are sinful or morally wrong. The person who slides and hits a parked vehicle while driving on a cold, icy winter day is described as "having been in an accident." It is clear that the harm to the parked vehicle would not have occurred but for the actions of the driver, yet the driver did not intend to cause the harm nor could the driver prevent the harm once the car began to slide on the ice.

Moral responsibility does not require that a person intended to do wrong or that harm would occur. The intent to do wrong clearly adds to the magnitude of the wrongdoing. The individual who commits wrong and intends to cause harm is judged to be deserving of a more severe consequence than the one who causes harm accidently, or without intent. However, in both cases, the person is judged to be responsible for the harm.

Punishment is often given to the person who has intentionally caused harm. It must not be confused with accepting responsibility for the consequences of the actions that caused the harm. Punishment involves retribution or a penalty while the consequences of an action naturally flow from the action for the purpose of correcting the harm caused by the action. It is not a punishment for the driver to pay for the repairs to the parked car after the accident. However, if it should be learned that the driver intended to damage the car (intentional harm), was driving recklessly (negligence), or was drunk (flagrant neglect), a just system is likely to demand punishment in addition to holding the person responsible for the consequences of such actions—he or she must repair the car.

Responsibility may also be assigned vicariously, that is, a person who could have or should have prevented the harm may be held responsible for the occurrence of the harm. The father who sits passively while a mother emotionally abuses their children or the mother who remains seemingly naive to sexual abuse occurring within the family is responsible for the occurrence of the harm. While such individuals do not have sole responsibility, they are responsible for their lack of action to prevent the harm. Mitigating circumstances influence decisions regarding punishment but do not relieve one from responsibility.

Excuses or explanations of why the harm occurred or why no action was taken to prevent the harm do not alter the assignment of responsibility. Adam's statement, "The woman you put here with me—she gave me some fruit from the tree, and I ate it" (Gen. 3:12), did not alter God's response to the transgression. Likewise, parents who had an abusive childhood and are now neglectful toward their children are still responsible for their actions. A description of mitigating circumstances may provide understanding and even compassion for the responsible person. However, an explanation does not justify or correct a wrong; rather, it merely puts into context the circumstances in which the wrong or harm occurred. The understanding of the context is important in determining if punishment is appropriate. This understanding does not relieve one from the consequences of one's actions.

Being created in God's image, we are angry at wrongdoing or harm and sense a need for both correction and retribution. Children at an early age often say, "That's not fair." The effects of living in a sinful world, whether intentional or not, are often not fair and all too frequently produce hurt and disconnection. Often, the pastoral counselor assists a counselee in discerning who is responsible. The determination of responsibility is necessary to address the guilt and resolve the shame. The issue of responsibility will determine the response to the guilt and identify the disconnection that produced the shame. It is only when responsibility for the disconnection has been determined that the pastoral counselor can proceed with strategies for resolution.

Resolving Moral Shame

The resolution of moral shame involves the following six steps:

1. Identification of responsibility
2. Acceptance of responsibility
3. Ownership of the resulting feelings
4. Confession
5. Forgiveness
6. Restitution/correction

Identifying that I am responsible for the sin or harm and the disconnection is necessary but not sufficient for acceptance of the responsibility. A person may be informed that he or she is responsible for a harm or disconnection and reply, "So what?" In a more subtle form, we may respond by minimizing the issue, as in "It doesn't matter," or make an excuse such as "I didn't mean to do it." Our culture offers no-fault divorce and no-fault insurance, which may serve as metaphors for our apparent desire for "no-fault living" in which personal responsibility is divorced from any consequences.

The husband who is having an affair may be able to acknowledge that his actions are wrong and that they cause disconnection in his marital relationship yet be unwilling to accept responsibility for his behavior. He may blame an uncaring wife, an overcontrolling mother, pressures at work, a mid-life crisis, or any other factor. Human beings seem to have no limit to their attempts to avoid responsibility. The acceptance of responsibility clarifies the situation, removes the blame from others, and identifies a way out, a means for resolution. In such a situation, the pastor is challenged to assist this man in identifying his guilt and accepting his personal responsibility. An often effective approach is the use of reflective listening, a strategy in which the counselor directs relevant information shared by the counselee back to the counselee in the form of a statement. A reflective statement can be used to both demonstrate to the counselee that the pastor has heard and has some understanding of what the counselee has shared. It also directs the counselee to attend to the content the pastor deems important. Often a reflective statement begins either explicitly or implicitly with the word "you," which facilitates connection. For example, the pastor may respond in the above situation with, "You hold your wife, mother, and pressures at work responsible for your affair." This statement may direct the person to further consider his or her beliefs. Reflective statements are most powerful and least threatening when they are stated and not formed as a question.

The acceptance of personal responsibility will result in the experience of emotional reactions. *Our emotions are simply reactions to perceived changes in our environment, relationships, or ourselves.* As such, they are neither good nor bad in the same way that blinking when exposed to a bright light is neither good nor bad.

Emotions are useful to us in three distinct ways. First, emotional reactions provide a great deal of information about what is occurring around or in us. The information available in our emotions allows us greater contact with reality and helps us cope. Table 2.1

Table 2.1
Emotions and Their Functions

Emotion	Purpose, Information Provided
joy, happiness	continue, this is good
acceptance, trust	affiliation, safety
anticipation	this is new, explore
surprise	unexpected, stop and get oriented, be alert
disgust, loathing	"this is poison," push away, reject
anger	something is wrong or I have been wronged; change something in my situation or within myself to correct the wrong
sadness	a loss has occurred; adjust to the loss, adapt, accept
fear	danger is present; change the situation, learn either to cope, or to escape from or avoid the situation
hurt	I have been harmed or abused; discontinue or avoid
shame	I am disconnected, I am not perfect; prompts reconnection and acceptance of our limitations, facilitating functioning well within reality; acceptance of real self

provides a summary of both the names of the primary emotionsand the information they provide. Second, emotions provide the energy necessary to cope in the present circumstances. For example, anger increases our energy to allow us to make changes while sadness decreases our energy and helps us let go of what we have lost. Third, the experiencing and release of our emotional reactions facilitate an internal reorganization within our psychological makeup, allowing us to accept what is new or different. The suppression of our emotions interferes with acceptance.

Many emotional reactions in addition to shame may occur when one accepts responsibility for sin, harm, or disconnection. For example, the person who has acknowledged lying to a friend is likely also to feel anger. He or she may be angry that the situation exists, that such a thing has happened, or that there are now consequences to his or her actions. Fear of the implications of such consequences may be present, as may fear of the unknown. In addition, the acceptance of personal responsibility may produce hurt, sadness, or disgust. Each of these emotional reactions requires both the identification of the emotion as well as the corresponding response to the emotion.

The presence of emotional reactions may indicate the acceptance of responsibility. Mere lip service does not move beyond the identification phase and will only suppress or deny the guilt and shame. In such situations, it is likely that the individual has walled off his or her ownership of responsibility with bitterness. Imposed shame (with its inherent inhibition) may block another person from progressing in the resolution of moral shame. In such circumstances the pastor will need to simultaneously address both the imposed and the moral shame issues, helping the counselee discern who is responsible and identifying the emotional reactions in each situation.

The acknowledgment of emotions by a pastor can have a profoundly positive effect in the counselee's life. Acknowledgment may occur through eye contact and a gentle nod, verbal statements indicating that it is permissible to have emotions, and either reflective or paraphrasing statements. A paraphrase, or a restatement of what has been shared in the pastor's words, can communicate acceptance and connection. The pastor's acknowledgment represents permission for the counselee to feel as well as to accept himself or herself.

Ownership of the emotional reactions following acceptance of responsibility leads to confession. If another person has been wronged, it is necessary in most circumstances to confess or acknowledge personal responsibility for wrongdoing to the other person. Confession of the wrongdoing to God is necessary to initiate reconnection with him. By its very nature, ownership involves confession to one's self.

Overt confession, or directly acknowledging the wrongdoing to the person involved, is not always beneficial. When a person does not know he or she has been wronged and it would cause harm to inform him or her, it may be best to not confess to that person. For example, harm may occur if a man would inform a female friend that he has been fantasizing about her and has used her as an object for lust. The supposed confession would likely cause further harm. However, this man does need to confess to himself, and to God, and to be accountable to another person. A pastoral counselor or someone who is mature in the faith may serve this purpose.

Confession is necessary for forgiveness to occur. It is forgiveness that provides the safety and the path for resolving our shame. In forgiveness, the opportunity for reconnection is possible, the shame may be released, and the relationship may be restored.

Forgiveness is not a mere forgetting, nor is it making excuses for the event or harm. Avoidance of conflict or compromise in one's moral position is not evidence of forgiveness. Events, behaviors, or words that have caused disconnection or harm have effects. Like a scar that results from a wound to the skin, the effects of the transgression remain even when there is forgiveness.

Forgiveness does involve a letting go, the canceling of a debt, a release, a pardon. Forgiveness is choosing not to punish someone even though justice might point in that direction. Created in God's image, we all experience righteous indignation when we have been wronged. Forgiveness is recognizing the wrong, holding the person who transgressed responsible for that wrong, and, in light of this, choosing not to punish. Forgiveness is the application of grace and truth. Truth is evidenced by the attribution of responsibility to the wrongdoer; grace is offered through the extension of the gift of love and release.

Forgiveness provides a bridge, a way back for the offender to be reconnected with the offended. The offender may request forgiveness; the offended may offer forgiveness. While many emotions are involved before, during, and after the forgiveness process, forgiveness is primarily cognitive. A decision is made, a commitment chosen, in which the offended person resolves to release his or her claims against the offender. The process of forgiveness then involves applying this choice to whatever circumstances may arise. The living of forgiveness challenges the forgiver to continue to release the offender each time there is a reminder of wrongdoing and to resolve the various emotional reactions that occur with each reminder.

Some perceived wrongs do not require forgiveness. Sometimes someone experiences shame and disconnection occurs and yet no guilt is apparent. A disconnection may occur between two people as the result of an honest difference, yet no one is responsible for a moral transgression. A misunderstanding of a message or a difference in preference may lead to a disconnection and the emotional reaction of shame. For example, a husband and wife may differ in their preferences either to talk or listen to music while riding together in a car. This is not a moral issue yet if the expectations were not clear or not accepted, one or both individuals could experience disconnection and thus shame. Such times call for forbearance rather than forgiveness. The pastor has a unique opportunity to provide teaching regarding the true nature of forgiveness. Such teaching can be interjected when the pastor identifies faulty beliefs that may contribute to unrealistic demands on and expectations of self or others. Such teaching may allow an opportunity to help counselees connect grace with their experience.

We are able to offer forgiveness because we have been forgiven by God. As it is not possible to give a gift you do not first possess, it is difficult to forgive someone else without first accepting forgiveness from the source of grace and truth, God himself.

As we are forgiven by God, we can forgive ourselves. The most difficult person to forgive may be yourself. We may be painfully aware of a transgression and its consequences. Reality may be all too evident to us. Yet God has taken on the punishment for us, forgiven us, and reached out to us in love. Self-forgiveness is the application of God's forgiveness to the self.

The power of forgiveness is liberating, providing a restored record (Jer. 31:34), restored love (Luke 7:47), restored health (2 Chron. 7:14), and restored relationships (Gen. 50:17; Ps. 32:1–5). As freeing as forgiveness is, forgiving is very difficult for us. Bitterness, vindictiveness, cynicism, ongoing hurt, and the separation from the offender can block the releasing of our rightful claims against the offender.

Genuine forgiveness does not remove the consequences of the wrongdoing. Thus, moral shame may only be resolved when there is restitution or correction. The person who repents turns away from the wrongdoing. The final process in the resolution of moral shame is restitution or correction.

A man backing out of his driveway hit his neighbor's parked car. He had no ill intent yet felt great shame as he heard the crash and then saw the damage. He knew he was responsible for the damage and felt anger at himself for not being more careful. At first, he asked himself, "Why did he park on the street today?" He quickly realized that didn't matter. He went to his neighbor, confessed he had damaged the car, and asked for forgiveness. The neighbor, surprised by the news, said "Yes, I will forgive you." The man then walked away, comfortable that he was forgiven and did not need to fear his neighbor's punishment.

Is this story complete? No, the consequences remain. The forgiveness offered by the neighbor releases the man from the threat of punishment yet the consequences of his error still need to be dealt with. The intent of the man is not relevant to the fact of the damage done to the car. The man is now called to complete the resolution of his shame by correcting the damage he caused. He pays to have the car repaired.

Not all consequences of a transgression or disconnection can be as easily corrected as fixing a car. Words spoken in the heat of anger, physical violence in a family, or sexual molestation cannot be taken back or sent to the shop and be corrected. Memories and emotional scars will remain. However, the offender's acceptance of responsibility and active resolution of the moral shame begin the process of correction and restitution. In addition, repentance and forgiveness offered and received should lead to changes in behavior that prevent a repetition of the transgression. A changed heart leads to changed behavior.

Moral shame provides the check and balance between respecting myself and my wants and respecting others. Moral shame serves as an internal self-regulator of behavior, inhibiting actions that have been paired with the emotion of shame. This powerful inhibitor, moral shame, is essential for our identity, relationships, daily coping, and relating to God. Sometimes, however, this emotional reaction occurs at times when a person has neither transgressed nor is responsible for the transgression. At those times, the individual is often tormented by a sense of shame that moral shame resolution is inadequate to relieve.

Imposed Shame

Imposed shame is the sense of disgrace, humiliation, self-contempt, or self-exposure with a longing to reconnect we feel following the perceived disconnection caused by another person's actions. Imposed shame is felt, for example, when an adult perceives he or she cannot live up to his or her parents' expectations, when children who live in abusive homes hate themselves, or when a woman who was sexually abused is disgusted with her needs and vulnerability. The disconnection is due to the behaviors for which some other person is responsible. By definition, a person experiences imposed shame when that person is innocent of wrongdoing and someone else is either guilty of a transgression against the first person and/or is responsible for the disconnection. The intent of the other person does not determine the experience of imposed shame. Shame occurs simply when a person perceives disconnection.

The Development of Imposed Shame

"Shame" can be used as a verb to describe the interpersonal process of acting in such a manner that causes another person to feel shame. The common phrases "shame on you" or "you should be ashamed" are examples of attempts to impose shame. Webster's defines the verbal use of shame as "to cause to feel shame, to bring dishonor or disgrace on, to force by making ashamed." The person who experiences the shame desires to be reconnected with the one who imposed the shame as the reconnection will bring relief from the painful emotional experience. Thus, the one who imposed shame, the imposer, has gained power or influence over the one who is experiencing the shame. Should the imposer not be available to reconnect for any reason, the perceived power or influence of that person increases. The need to connect and the desire for relief from the emotional pain of shame are very strong motivators.

Shame may be imposed in many ways. The person responsible for the disconnection, the imposer, may or may not be aware of the disconnection. Neither the imposer's awareness nor intent is necessary for a person to experience imposed shame.

All types of shame are experienced initially in the same way. The feeling state does not identify who is responsible for the disconnection or transgression. Often the person who feels the shame confuses the painful emotional reactions with a thought or judgment of personal guilt. This transformation, aided by our common use of the phrase "I feel guilty," contributes to great confusion about who is guilty. The question of guilt is central to the resolution of the shame experience and a misattribution of guilt may block relief from the shame. We cannot forgive ourselves for something someone else did, nor can we forgive someone else for something we did.

The disabling effects of imposed shame are most evident in those situations in which there is a failure of the shaming person to reconnect with the one who was shamed. In such circumstances, emotions, thoughts, needs, talents, and even behaviors may become paired with shame and the person lives a chronically inhibited and painful existence. Unable to obtain relief from this painful emotion, such an individual appears to be under the power of the imposer.

The need to connect leaves all of us vulnerable to imposed shame. Simply being ignored, neglected, or abandoned by someone can produce intense feelings of shame. In addition to the painful feelings, thoughts such as *Why am I not good enough?* may occur. Children who are neglected or ignored often feel unlovable, unworthy, and insecure. The individual who feels the shame longs to reconnect with the person who has ignored, neglected, or abandoned him or her. Such individuals may think, *If only they would love me, then I could love myself.*

Misattribution of responsibility, or falsely blaming another for one's wrongdoing, distress, or general circumstances, produces imposed shame. The tired father who yells at the children and says, "You drive me crazy," or the wife who tells her husband, "It's your fault that I feel this way" are improperly placing the responsibility for their feelings and well-being on either their children or spouse.

In a similar manner, the denial of responsibility by one person tends to impose shame on those who interact with that person. Parents who do not fulfill their parental responsibilities inadvertently put pressure on their children to assume those duties and roles. In such circumstances, the oldest child often becomes a "little adult" and may seem very responsible. At a young age this child may find that the best chance at connecting with the parent is to act responsibly and assume parental duties. As this young person is still a child, he or she experiences some failure in managing these adult duties. In addition, normal child needs, such as needing to be protected and nurtured, may be ignored and go unmet. The child strives to be very responsible in order to obtain connection with the parent. As adults, such individuals tend to assume much responsibility yet experience self-doubt, depression, and difficulty with vulnerability and intimacy.

A violation of the boundaries between any two people can impose shame. This is especially relevant in the parent-child relationship. Children define their identity and self-worth through their relationship with their parents (this will be further addressed in Chapter 4). When the parent violates the needs of the child, the child experiences disconnection. The child still longs to connect with the parent for he or she needs the parent (physically, emotionally, mentally, and spiritually). The painful violations of abuse do not erase the child's need to connect. Rather, the child, left in imposed shame, often idealizes the abusing parent even more. The disconnection fuels the perceived need of the child for that parent.

Social workers are at times baffled when they attempt to remove children from abusive homes. Expecting children to be happy to be protected from the abuse, they often encounter children cling-ing to the abusive parent. These children feel intense shame at the prospect of being further disconnected from their parents and, in an attempt to ward off the pain of shame, cling to their parents. In a similar manner, police officers who attempt to arrest a husband who has been physically violent with his wife often discover that the wife objects to the arrest and may even attack the officers. Again, the disconnection from the husband would be intensified if he were arrested and the resulting imposed shame would be more painful and seemingly more difficult to resolve.

Adult men and women who have been abused by their parents often are the most vocal defenders and protectors of those parents. The parents are placed on a pedestal. Great qualities are ascribed to them; they seemingly can do no wrong. These adults have great difficulty holding their parents responsible for anything; rather, they attribute any form of disconnection or shame to themselves. The parents are experienced as basically good, the self as basically bad. Even thinking about the abuse that occurred may result in more intense shame and such self-statements as "I must really be a bad person to have such thoughts." Acknowledging the abuse makes real the disconnection and thus the shame. To have an illu-sion of connection and to attempt to minimize the pain of the shame, the person who has been abused often sacrifices himself or herself to protect the parent.

People abuse each other in many ways. Emotional, physical, mental, and sexual forms of abuse all are damaging to identity and to self. They are an insult to the Creator. Being abused produces fear, righteous indignation, rage, and shame. Abuse is a violent form of disconnection.

Shame may be imposed in more subtle ways. People who learn that what happens to them is not related to what they do often become fatalistic, depressed, maybe even hopeless. Psychologists refer to this as learned helplessness. Early in a child's development, there is a need for the parent to respond first to the child's sounds, then eye movements, and later the child's requests. Children need to learn that they can impact their world, that they make a differ-ence and can be seen and heard. In some families all behaviors are rewarded and praised; in other families all behaviors are punished;

and in others the child's behaviors are randomly rewarded or punished. All three scenarios will result in imposed shame as children experience disconnection from their parents as well as their own behavior.

In many seemingly "good" families, ego-boundaries between parent and child become blurred and confused. Emotional incest may occur in which the parent uses the child to meet certain emotional needs in a manner resembling a surrogate spouse. The child may appear to have a "special relationship" with the parent. In reality, this relationship has denied the developmental needs of the child and thus has paired shame with his or her needs for privacy, independence, and autonomy.

As imposed shame is painful and people are strongly motivated to find relief by reconnecting with the imposer, many individuals and institutions impose shame as a means of exerting control. The teacher who belittles a student, the coach who insults and ridicules his athletes, and the pastor who only focuses on conviction of sin all are eliciting a shame response and are likely to see increased compliance. Such conforming of behavior comes at a great price, however.

Imposed shame can cripple people, inhibiting them so that they appear to be mere shells. The inhibitory effects of shame leave people bound up, unable to feel, and afraid to think for themselves. Distortions of reality, confusion, concrete thinking, and the loss of the ability to abstract occur with imposed shame. Relationships are also impaired. The unmet need to connect leaves the shamed person highly dependent or fearful of others. Wanting to be loved, he or she is seemingly unable to receive love. God is often experienced as judgmental, harsh, and distant. Self-contempt and a disgust or even loathing of the self are not uncommon. Thoughts of being loved may occur but the feelings do not correspond. A failure to reconnect with the one who imposed the shame leaves the hurting person feeling alone, unlovable, and helpless.

Resolving Imposed Shame

The process of resolving imposed shame is summarized in Table 2.2. Upon determining that shame is present, the pastor is challenged to identify with the counselee the type of shame which will determine the resolution strategy. As with moral shame, the resolution of imposed shame begins with the attribution of responsibility. Many questions arise: Who is responsible for the disconnection? Has there been a transgression, a wrongdoing, a sin? Or is the disconnection due to a mere difference of opinion? What am I responsible for in the disconnections that have left me feeling shame?

Table 2.2
The Resolution of Imposed Shame

1. Reattribute responsibility for the disconnection
1.1. Hold self responsible when appropriate.
1.2. Hold other person responsible for his or her part.
2. Identify, own, and resolve all emotional reactions.
3. Use anger to reestablish boundaries.
4. Learn to accept love from someone.
5. Apply love to self.
6. Confront the imposer (in person or symbolically).
6.1. Confess personal responsibility.
6.2. Identify imposer's responsibility.
7. Forgiveness.
7.1. Of and from the other.
7.2. Of and from self.
7.3. From God.
8. Rebuild the relationship in truth and grace.

The experience of shame is imposed shame when the other person is responsible for the disconnection. The same guidelines outlined for determining responsibility for moral shame should be used for imposed shame. In parent-child relationships in which the child is young at the time of the incident the parent is responsible. Young children are not nor can they be responsible for the acts of adults. Young children cannot make adults connect or disconnect, be angry or happy, love them or abuse them. Rather, young children respond to the adults. As children age and mature, they are increasingly held more accountable for their actions. The parents remain responsible for how they parented the child; adult children are responsible for how they cope with what they received and how they now live.

However, even adults are not responsible for all of their experience. Adults are responsible for their behavior, for how they live, for the choices they make, and for how they cope. Adults may not be responsible for what they have learned, memories that they have, emotional reactions to those memories, and other scars from childhood. Adults are responsible for how they cope with the scars but may not be responsible for the wounds that produced the scars.

The attribution of responsibility involves assigning culpability to both the imposer and the self. In some situations, such as a woman who was raped, the guilt is clear and the rapist is held responsible. The shame felt by the woman is due to the guilt of the rapist. Should family members respond to the news of the rape by being emotionally distant or telling her that she needs to put it behind her and never talk about it, the resulting shame would again be imposed shame. She would feel shame because of the disconnection caused by others.

Other situations are more complicated. Consider a man who was reared in a family in which the father was an alcoholic and both verbally and physically abusive to the family members while the mother was passive and appeared to be powerless yet protected her husband's reputation. In his present functioning, this man struggles with difficulties in trusting others and allowing himself to be vulnerable, and experiences intense anger toward his wife. In addition, he does not experience God as loving but rather as harsh and judgmental. This man describes himself as unlovable and a failure as a husband, father, and man.

In such a situation, the pastoral counselor is challenged to help this man discriminate between what he is responsible for (such as his anger at and behavior toward his wife) and those things he is not responsible for (such as having learned to not trust). While he is not responsible for learning not to trust, he is responsible for his present behavior toward his wife, others, and himself. He is *not* responsible for being taught that he is unworthy yet *is* now responsible for his own self-care.

The appropriate assignment of responsibility is critically important for two reasons. First, one cannot forgive oneself for something for which one is not responsible. In the above example, the man cannot forgive himself for being abused. He did not abuse; rather, it happened to him at the hand of his father. Forgiveness is only possible when the guilty party is held liable.

Second, forgiveness must include an examination of our own responsibility in the matter. Jesus stated that we need to examine the plank in our own eye before being concerned about the speck in another's eye (Matt. 7:3). This man could hold his father responsible and blame his father for all of his current problems. The person who does this is quickly stuck, unable to make changes in his or her life as the other person is given the power. As this man owns his part, accepts responsibility for his actions, he can free himself of the corresponding guilt and experience increased self-control. Moral shame must be resolved as well as imposed shame.

At times people have difficulty identifying that someone else is responsible for the shame they feel. The person whose spouse demands absolute perfection may feel shame and judge himself or herself inadequate because of the impossibility of living up to the spouse's expectations. To help clarify the situation, the pastor may ask the counselee to imagine that someone else has told the counselee's story. The pastor can then paraphrase the story presented by the counselee and then ask, "What would *you* say to this person?" It is often helpful to objectify a situation when attributing responsibility. Identifying who is responsible often involves deep and intense emotional reactions. These emotional reactions often present difficulties for the shamed person due to early learning in which shame-affect binds were formed. Now to feel an emotion such as anger or hurt produces further feelings of shame. For many, the question of responsibility has been too dangerous to ask. They have confused feeling shame with being guilty; they fear it is disrespectful to think or speak unkindly about a parent, or experience more shame as they say out loud what they have known before. Fear, hurt, sadness, and anger often result from recognizing that another person's behavior produced the disconnection that caused the shame. At such a time, the person may come to a very important realization: "I'm not unlovable or bad; rather, I have been hurt or wronged and that's not right!"

In complicated situations, this process of attributing responsibility and experiencing the emotional reactions proceeds in a cyclical manner. Some areas of responsibility are delineated, strong emotional reactions result, some acceptance occurs, and then the individual recognizes a need to further define other related issues. This process may consume much time as the person sorts through what has happened and attributes responsibility.

Anger has a necessary and critical role in the resolution of imposed shame. The Scriptures attribute anger to God. We possess the same capacity, and it is useful to help us determine when a wrong has occurred and to have sufficient energy to change the wrong. If the wrong is changed, the anger is released. We often feel angry when our boundaries have been violated, when our expectations do not match our experience, and when we have been wronged. When we attribute responsibility and recognize that someone else has imposed shame on us, we respond with anger.

The emotion of anger is often present before a person is aware of what is troubling him or her. Accepting the fact of the anger and asking "What am I angry about?" helps define the problem. Once the problem is defined and responsibility assigned with regard to guilt, the anger makes it possible to clarify boundaries. As children are angry when toys are taken from them, adults feel angry when they have been wronged. Both of these responses mirror our Creator's anger and righteous indignation at sin.

Paul has instructed us: "In your anger do not sin. Do not let the sun go down while you are still angry" (Eph. 4:26). We are to resolve our anger. Suppression or denial of anger only delays anger's effects and builds bitterness. Resolution of anger requires change. Often, that change occurs within us as we accept what has happened.

Acceptance is more than verbal acknowledgment of something. It involves an emotional embracing and a release of hopes and expectations for or claims against someone. The man who accepts his father comes to grip with the reality of who this man is (or was), his strengths as well as his faults, what he has done, and what he has failed to do. In like manner, to accept ourselves requires the same awareness of who we are, the good, the bad, and the ugly. Acceptance involves seeing ourselves and others as God does.

To see ourselves as God sees us includes his love for us. When we are under the influence of imposed shame, accepting love from others is difficult if not impossible. The person who is covered with imposed shame feels the pain of disconnection, self-contempt, and isolation and is unable to receive love. Others' attempts to extend love may be misinterpreted and pushed away. The messages that occurred in the disconnection are paired with the emotion of shame and replayed automatically. Messages given either overtly or covertly maintain the imposed shame. It is as if the imposer is continually present, informing the person of the disconnection and that he or she is unlovable.

Learning to receive love from others counters the shaming messages. If someone is able to love me, then I may be loveable. If someone connects with me, then I am able to connect. The acceptance of love from another contradicts the messages and validates the person's anger at the messages and the imposer. The person in imposed shame is shown to be loveable. In this way, the pastoral counselor and others can reflect God's love to the person trapped in imposed shame. The messages of the imposer are proven wrong by the love.

We cannot give what we have not received. Receiving love disputes the messages of worthlessness or self-contempt. Seeing beyond the pain of the imposed shame, we become able to apply the love to ourselves. We now have something to give and can move toward fulfilling the great commandment of loving God with the whole self and our neighbor as ourselves.

With a more realistic perception of self, acceptance of his or her own emotional reactions, and understanding and acceptance of who is responsible for which parts of the disconnection, a person is ready to address the imposer. This meeting between the imposer and the one who carried the imposed shame is often feared. Whether the meeting occurs in person or symbolically, the person who has experienced imposed shame needs to share his or her understanding of the situation. In the imposer's actual or symbolic presence, the shamed person needs to state what has happened, who is responsible for each aspect of what has occurred, and confess any sin (if there is guilt). At the same time, the shamed person holds the imposer responsible for what the imposer has done. The imposed shame can then be released to the imposer.

A pastor may facilitate a symbolic meeting with the imposer by using the empty chair technique. The counselee may address an empty chair as if the imposer were seated in the room. Thoughts and feelings regarding the imposer can then be expressed. If judged to be helpful, the pastor may do a role-play, taking the part of the imposer and thus providing the counselee with an opportunity to dialogue with "the imposer." Ideally the person guilty for imposing shame will ask for forgiveness; and the shamed person can release the imposer from his or her guilt. The shamed person can choose to offer forgiveness to the imposer whether or not the imposer requests it. The imposer does not have the power to block the shamed person from forgiving him or her. The shamed person can imitate the forgiveness and grace of God that come to us even before we realize our guilt and have a sense of moral shame.

At times the imposer denies responsibility. The shamed person is confronted with a choice: Whom do I believe? The pastoral counselor can help prepare the person for this possibility if the shamed person chooses to meet with and confront the imposer. It may be that the shamed person has had inadequate information to realistically determine responsibility. At such times, the shamed person can listen and discriminate among new information, explanations of why certain things happened, and excuses, none of which alter responsibility. To tell someone after an accident that "I didn't mean to run into your car" clarifies motive but does not change the fact of responsibility for the damage.

The imposer may not care that the wrong occurred, may conclude that the issue is not important, may be angry at being held responsible, or may disconnect further in an attempt to impose further shame and thus inhibit the process. At such a time, the shamed person needs to hold on to what is true and receive support and love from others.

The imposer may have yet another response. Convicted of sin, the imposer may accept responsibility and apologize. Sometimes conviction occurs immediately; in other circumstances much time passes before the imposer returns and requests forgiveness. Again, it is the shamed person's responsibility to forgive the imposer whether or not the imposer acknowledges forgiveness.

Forgiveness allows the shamed person to be released from the power of the imposer as well as from moral shame. Forgiveness permits the beginning of a new relationship between the shamed person and the imposer. This new relationship can be built in truth, with honest mutual acceptance in the relationship. However, forgiveness does not erase consequences nor does it destroy memory. The new relationship, built on grace and truth, is characterized by respect for all involved.

At times this mutual respect allows for increased openness and intimacy. Releasing shame grants the opportunity for people to know each other, to come out of hiding, and to heal. However, in other circumstances it is neither safe nor wise to become more vulnerable to the imposer. The woman living with a physically abusive husband who denies wrongdoing and who hears threats of further beatings "if I ever hear another word of this" is not safe. She is not witholding love by seeking her own safety. If anyone is responsible for disconnection, it is the abusive husband. Acknowledgment of this by the pastor, given the role and authority of his position, may be helpful in granting permission for the counselee to establish appropriate boundaries.

Many carry the pain of imposed shame long after the imposer has died. In these cases, the discussion about responsibility will clearly need to be symbolic. Although the imposer is dead, the living person maintains a relationship with the imposer through memory. A new relationship in memory is then necessary, a relationship built on grace and truth. This new relationship in memory will alter the shamed person's attitude toward not only the imposer but also toward himself or herself. As we are able realistically to accept ourselves and others we become more open to God.

Natural Shame

Human beings have experienced natural shame since the fall. Not only did Adam and Eve immediately experience moral shame for their transgression, but they were forever changed in their capacity to relate to God, to each other, and to their environment. They now possessed a sin nature, a tendency toward wrongdoing and selfishness, an inability to be perfectly connected. From that time on we have been confronted with the knowledge that no matter how hard we try, we still fall short of the mark.

Natural shame is often experienced at times of contemplation, or self-reflection, and at times spent alone. It may be evident at those times in which plans are considered, goals are reviewed, or the state of one's life is considered. Natural shame may be experienced when we are frustrated, disappointed, or let down and recognize that we have done our best. Acknowledging that we cannot give any more, try any harder, or perform any better may be a threatening experience if our worth or acceptability depends upon our performance.

Our culture with its relativistic values has attempted to deny natural shame. We are told that human beings are good and only do "bad" things because they have been victimized. Even so, it is clear there are no absolutely good people. To account for this, the environment has been blamed for the "bad" behaviors of these "good" people. Rather than accept our natural shame, the culture labels people as "victims" and removes them from responsibility for their actions, thus confusing being victimized with being a victim. The victim now has an identity. This produces people who perceive themselves as both helpless and entitled, waiting and demanding to be satisfied by others.

Our culture has denied natural shame because we do not like to identify problems for which we do not have answers. It is threatening to acknowledge a sin nature if there is no cure for it. How dangerous it would be to identify a need for God if we are invested in believing that there is nothing greater than ourselves. Others are unaware of their natural shame as they are constantly imprisoned by the pain of imposed shame and are never free of the judgments of the imposers of shame. Both the denial of and the inability to perceive natural shame lead to distortions in the perception of the self and others.

The Value of Natural Shame

Natural shame brings into our awareness our need for something greater than the self. My fallibility, my inability to be perfect, identifies my limits and leaves me with a longing for something more. As such, the experience of natural shame is a reality contact, reminding us of our boundaries. Our inadequacies and inherent deficiencies are evident. It is when we experience natural shame that we realize our need for God, our intrinsic inability to be fully self-sufficient.

Furthermore, I am not the only one who has needs. Others are not fully self-sufficient and are imperfect. All human beings, including those we may long to connect with but are unavailable, are flawed. The realization and acceptance of natural shame is a great leveling experience. All people have a sin problem.

In a moment of apparent reflection on natural shame, the apostle Paul wrote "I do not understand what I do. For what I want to do I do not do, but what I hate I do" (Rom. 7:15). Our best efforts are insufficient. Our attempts to be perfect only demonstrate our imperfection. For some, this leads to despair and self-contempt. In light of the gospel, these realizations lead to a realistic self-acceptance, humility, and dependence on our heavenly Father.

Resolving Natural Shame

Just as a young son cannot make a father reconnect, we are unable to make ourselves reconnect with what we have lost. Throughout human history, people have attempted to make the reconnection themselves. From Cain's sacrifice, to the tower of Babel, to the Pharisees' adherence to the letter of the law, to modern legalism, people have focused on doing the right thing, on their performance, rather than letting go and accepting God's offer for reconnection. As natural shame does not result from our doing but from our being, reconnection does not occur by our doing but by our receiving.

God, in the person of Jesus Christ, has reached toward us and offered us reconnection. Since human efforts to reconnect with him are insufficient, leaving humans in their sin and shame, God has reached out to us. When by the grace of God people accept God's offer of redemption and justification, their natural shame is resolved. A new creature exists that has the capacity to directly relate to God and a new capacity to relate to others and the self. Their guilt has been resolved, the attribution of responsibility has been clarified, and they have an option of reconnection.

Daily living will still disrupt the connection as sin continues to influence our behavior and experience. However, the power of sin is broken and rather than despair, the believer can repent, again acknowledge dependence on God, and experience reconnection. Shame is released.

Understanding and acceptancing natural shame is liberating. To be free from the pressure to perform or to be released from the demands to be perfect is possible when we accept our own limitations and needs and allow God to redeem. We come to understand that while we are not sufficient, our heavenly Father is and we can rest in this knowledge and feel safe, secure, and loved.

Application of the Threefold Model

This threefold model of shame provides the pastoral counselor with a tool for resolving shame and guilt problems. The process may start at different places. If the emotion of shame has been identified, the question becomes which type of shame. Since shame simply feels like shame, the type is identified by determining who is responsible for the disconnection. The pastoral counselor then helps implement relevant resolution strategies.

At times the pastoral counselor may meet a person who lacks shame feelings but is clearly guilty of a transgression. Some people protect themselves from experiencing any shame because they are in a chronic state of imposed shame and fear they cannot carry any more pain and accusations of guilt. This may appear to be either apathy or ignorance or take the form of a seared conscience or a hardened heart. In extreme forms, these individuals are labeled psychopaths. Here moral shame must be felt and imposed shame must be resolved.

Others are truly ignorant of either the standards of right and wrong and thus have no sense of moral violation. Still others continue to assert their wills and choose to transgress. In both cases, such people will benefit from being shown that they are responsible for their transgressions as the first step in resolving their shame and guilt problem.

At times the pastoral counselor is confronted with a person who is not aware of a specific problem but has a more general sense of disconnection. Or the disconnection is greater than what is understood. In defining the problem, it may become apparent that the individual is disconnected from God. The experience of natural shame, not yet understood, has prompted him or her to seek help. At such times the pastoral counselor has the privilege of introducing such a person to the reality of the heavenly Father.

$$3$$

Guilt and Shame
in Christian Belief

Biblical Descriptions of Guilt and Shame

Christians and non-Christians alike recognize the reality of guilt and shame. Different cultures and religions will, of course, analyze the problems with their own unique twists and nuances. The Christian must react to guilt and shame from the framework of belief that is based on the Word—Christ as the living Word, and the Scriptures as the expressed Word of God. As we look at guilt and shame in Christian belief we will examine some of the biblical descriptions, the biblical notion of conscience, and the way of salvation as the solution to guilt and shame.

The biblical passages studied in this chapter may be the kind of texts that the pastoral counselor puts in the hands of those to whom he or she speaks. Pastoral counseling is empowered by the judicious use of the Bible. It would hardly be an exaggeration to say that guilt and shame appear on virtually every page of the Bible. The pastoral counselor can give to those he or she counsels a wealth of biblical material that speaks directly to these issues. The Scriptures provide both a detailed analysis of the roots of the human predicament, and how the God of truth and grace has provided a complete and total solution to that predicament.

When dealing with people who have severe problems with shame pastors will frequently find some who say that they have a hard time reading the Bible. Either it seems empty to them, or they end up feeling such overwhelming shame that they turn away. Pastors should not be surprised and should be careful how they react to people who say, "I haven't been able to have a devotional life for a long time now. I can't read the Bible and I can hardly bring myself to pray." What is happening to such people is that an inner disposition of self-condemnation is causing them to read every possible external signal as rejection. *Why didn't my boss smile at me this morning? I must have done something wrong. Why isn't my spouse happy? Why isn't my kid doing well in school? How can I possibly stand before God when the Bible so overwhelmingly condemns me as a sinner?*

The pastoral counselor can be ready with specific passages of Scripture that fill in the gaps of counselees' understanding of God or themselves.

Beginnings

Mark Twain said that human beings are the only animals that blush—or need to. Yet the story of Adam and Eve teaches that human nature, as God created it, is capable of goodness and wholeness. There was a time when human beings did not blush, and did not need to. "The man and his wife were both naked, and they felt no shame" (Gen. 2:25). The opening chapters of the Bible teach about innocence and guilt, about being unashamed and dropping into shame. Though there was law ("you must not eat"), there was as yet no transgression, no guilt, no shame.

There is in this archetype of human experience an anatomy of *forensic* realities (innocence giving way to guilt) and *experiential* realities (wholeness giving way to shame). The root of guilt, sin, is not simply stepping over a defined boundary. In the story of Eden we see sin as a violation of law, grace, and position.

   Disobedience to divine law is a blatant disrespect for that order
in the universe that is our only hope for stability and security. It is
to reject the structures whereby God directs us into healthy living.
The sin in the garden was also a violation of grace. It was an act of
robbery in a time of abundance. The Genesis account repeatedly
emphasizes God's act of grace in providing the garden ("God
blessed them. . . . God said, 'I give you every seed-bearing plant . . .
and every tree. . . . They will be yours for food'" [1:28–29]; "the LORD
God planted a garden . . . and there he put the man he had formed"
[2:8]; "you are free to eat from any tree in the garden" [2:16]). Thus,
the taking of forbidden fruit was an insult to the abundant provision of God. The sin in Eden also represents a violation of position.
Innocence meant not knowing evil—which, ironically was used to
tempt Adam and Eve ("you're missing something, God is holding
back, you can know all things and be like him!") The temptation to
reach for the fruit and so become like God is all the more tragic
because Adam and Eve already were like God, in a proper, derived
sense. Guilt began with human beings desiring to be more than
what they should be, and ended with them being less than what
they were intended to be.
   As an anatomy of the experience of shame, this story goes on to
depict a terrible disconnectedness in the world: human beings disconnected from God, from each other, and even from themselves.
The man and the woman immediately withdraw from God:

> Then the man and his wife heard the sound of the LORD God as he
> was walking in the garden in the cool of the day, and they hid from
> the LORD God among the trees of the garden. But the LORD God called
> to the man, "Where are you?"
>   He answered, "I heard you in the garden, and I was afraid because
> I was naked; so I hid." (3:8–10)

   In the modern world we tend to think the first question is "Where
is God?" The more original question, however, belongs to God:
"Where is man?" What happened? Why are you hiding? Obscurity
is a game human beings play with God, not the other way around.
Shame does not exist in a vacuum. When people experience shame,
they have a sense of disgrace about something and before some-

one. It is from the displeasure of God that Adam and Eve hid themselves, and so it is with everyone who is guilty but neglects going with a contrite heart to the offended. They end up more estranged. Shame snuffs out the living warmth of relationships. Each transgression requires another subterfuge to cover the flaw.

Thus, the pastoral counselor can expect to find a whole network of relational issues in a person struggling with shame and guilt. One's relationship with God is affected, and thereafter almost any other human relationship. If hiding from the truth has been a coping pattern then the person may have highly developed, even unconscious ways of masking reality.

In the Genesis account the disconnectedness between the human beings shows up immediately. In response to God's inquiry concerning their actions, Adam employs a tactic that will become the all-too-common pattern of many people convicted of their guilt: blaming. "The woman whom you put here with me—she gave me some fruit from the tree, and I ate it" (3:12). Though we are not given a blow-by-blow description of the domestic life of the original couple, we do get a graphic depiction of human estrangement in the conflict of the two sons, Cain and Abel. Cain has his own problems with God, and presents an unacceptable offering. God inquires of this bitter man who has already succumbed to shame while doing nothing constructive about it, "Why are you angry? Why is your face downcast?" With his face turned down in shame, Cain made the biggest mistake of his life by lashing out at his brother.

What, in the story of Adam and Eve, should we make of the connection between shame and nakedness? While the story does point to physical nakedness, we need not assume that that is all that is going on with Adam and Eve. Our physical selves can be the external manifestation of all of what we are. The way we view ourselves on the inside can show itself by how we might preen and primp our bodies. When Adam and Eve covered their bodies, there was a message there about the soul. We cannot always pinpoint it in our own thinking, but there is so often that sense that something is missing in us, we are not what we should be, we are ugly, we must cover up. Human beings have been covering up ever since.

Pastoral counselors should not neglect the power of biblical stories in the counseling process. In the story of Eden are elements that are universal and easily grasped. It establishes the created goodness of man, the nature of temptation and transgression, the state of guilt, and the cowering experience of shame. It is everybody's story.

The Law

The forensic issue of guilt comes to the fore when progressive revelation arrives at the law. The law of Moses is really an extended definition of the meaning of guilt and innocence. Here the emphasis is on the legal, forensic issues because law by its nature is a definition of boundaries of right and wrong. When is a person truly guilty before God? When innocent? How can someone resolve the problem of guilt? What is the role of confession? Who is going to judge what is right and wrong, and how? These are some of the key questions addressed by the definitions set out in Exodus, Leviticus, and Deuteronomy.

The objectivity of guilt is demonstrated in the notion of unintentional sin. "If a member of the community sins unintentionally and does what is forbidden in any of the LORD's commands, he is guilty" (Lev. 4:27). This is an almost scandalous statement for modern people to hear. We assume that intention is at the heart of guilt and innocence. A person is not guilty if he or she injured someone accidentally or committed a crime while in a mentally crippled state. The emphasis that we get in the Old Testament law, however, is that when something happens that is wrong, it is wrong. If this seems merciless and senseless, it should be pointed out that the law allowed for a complete and accessible solution to the problem of unintentional sin in the sacrificial system, and that the real sanctions in the law were applied to intentional sin. Nevertheless, such statements impress on us that we must view our race as fallen, fallible, and imperfect. When something bad happens, intended or not, it is bad.

Thus sprang forth in Israel some of its most characteristic institutions: the courts of judgment, the priesthood (for atonement for sin), and the law itself. Instead of living by the human instincts of revenge and feud, there was an objective code. It had clarity, specificity, and universality. To help interpret the code there were the courts: "When men have a dispute, they are to take it to court and the judges will decide the case, acquitting the *innocent* and condemning the *guilty*" (Deut. 25:1).

In modern Western society we assume such structures. We count on the law and the courts for our protection. But by no means has the rule of law always been a characteristic of human societies. When God revealed his law through Moses, the human race was being given a fundamental lesson in rightness in living. If we do assume such principles today, it is only because we stand on the foundation that the Judeo-Christian heritage has provided. To discard the objective principles of guilt and innocence is like trying to build a house with no foundation.

It is not only sociologists and pollsters who see such trends. A pastoral counselor at any time may be speaking to someone whose house is built on the sand of ethical relativity. There are plenty of people in our society whose parental upbringing and social setting were nearly devoid of moral instruction. They simply cannot fathom the concept of objective guilt. Perhaps they know that if you break the law you may have to pay a fine or spend time in jail, but the problem then is having gotten caught, not having done wrong.

The Prophets

Later still in the progress of revelation, we get further elaboration on guilt and shame in the teachings of the prophets. Sometimes their oracles reinforce earlier teaching about God's inherent interest in justice and rightness. In the words of Nahum (1:3): "The LORD is slow to anger and great in power; the LORD will not leave the guilty unpunished. His way is in the whirlwind and the storm, and clouds are the dust of his feet."

In other ways they refine the Old Testament understanding of guilt. For instance, there is always the question of corporate guilt. Sometimes Israel suffered consequences as a whole because of the sin of some, like the sin of Achan (Josh. 7). On the other hand, we know that responsibility for specific instances of transgression produce guilt for the individuals involved. There had been a proverb, Ezekiel says, "the fathers eat sour grapes, and the children's teeth are set on edge." But such an idea is misleading. "The soul who sins is the one who will die. The son will not share the guilt of the father, nor will the father share the guilt of the son. The righteousness of the righteous man will be credited to him, and the wickedness of the wicked will be charged against him" (18:20). Here is a crystal clear definition of personal culpability.

Apostolic Teaching

One of the interesting developments in New Testament teaching relates to the issue of misplaced guilt, or imposed shame. It arises out of the experience of suffering, first in Jesus, and then in his followers. Peter says it clearly when he writes: "If you suffer as a Christian, *do not be ashamed*, but praise God that you bear that name" (1 Peter 4:16). Much of the Book of Acts is the story of a falsely accused man, the apostle Paul. During one of his trials he takes his stand on the objectivity of law as it relates to guilt and innocence: "If, however, I *am guilty* of doing anything deserving death, I do not refuse to die. But if the charges brought against me by these Jews are not true, no one has the right to hand me over to them. I appeal to Caesar!" (25:11). Though ridiculed and persecuted, he writes to the Roman Christians: "I am *not ashamed* of the gospel, because it is the power of God for the salvation of everyone who believes: first for the Jew, then for the Gentile" (Rom. 1:16). What an irony that Christians from the very start have borne the message of the righteousness of God, only to be accused of being wrong for doing so.

No different is the situation of the contemporary Christian who must carefully interpret the experience of shame and come up with true discernment of the fine lines between guilt and innocence. The pastoral counselor is indeed an interpreter. The counselee who is confused about being guilty or not is probably listening to a multitude of voices—voices from the past (parents, teachers, religious educators) as well as the present (friends, peers, social norms). It seems incredible that some accusers will actually take something good and right and call it bad and wrong ("you should stay home with me instead of going to church," "you just go to make me look bad," "your spiritual life is just your way of trying to impress other people"). But it happens all the time. Such people need to know that they are not alone in having received such unfair criticism.

The Christian Understanding of Conscience

The themes thus far mentioned in this chapter are objective issues (unless, like many people in the modern world, you assume that there is no objectivity to what is right or wrong, good or bad). The Scriptures also address some of the subjective issues, the way we experience shame, the way our hearts interpret guilt. The inner voice that God has given as a special gift to us as creatures uniquely created in his image clearly identifies us as different than all the rest of creation. Our moral sensitivity ennobles us, for it reveals a capacity to sense things that give meaning to life. Because human beings speak in terms of ought and ought not they show the capacity to discern what the good life is.

Most often we call this moral sensitivity conscience. Ask people to come up with an image of the conscience, and they might picture one or two impish figures sitting on one's shoulders, whispering suggestions of right and wrong in either ear. We know what it is, mostly because we are aware when we have a "bad conscience," which is just another way of saying we feel ashamed.

Martin Luther's powerful personal story is that of the transformation of a conscience (and with it the consciences of multitudes who would change the course of Western history). Writing years later, he reflected back on his days as a young, troubled monk:

> For, however irreproachably I lived as a monk, I felt myself before God to be a sinner with a most unquiet conscience, nor could I be confident that I had pleased him with my satisfaction [i.e. penance]. I did not love, nay, rather I hated, this righteous God who punished sinners, and if not with tacit blasphemy, certainly with huge murmurings I was angry with God, saying: "as though it really were not enough that miserable sinners should be eternally damned with original sin and have all kinds of calamities laid upon them by the law of the Ten commandments, God must go and add sorrow upon sorrow and even through the gospel itself bring his justice and wrath to bear!" I raged in this way with a wildly aroused and disturbed conscience. (Cited in Pauck 1961)

This man "with a most unquiet conscience" worried that if he neglected to confess a single sin that God's condemnation would rest on his shoulders. He trembled when he first served communion as a priest because of the possibility of defiling the body and blood of Christ. He was told by his superior in his order that he should come back to confession when he had some *real* sins to confess. But worst of all, he had a distorted view of God. He had no grasp of the grace and love of God because he could only see God as a holy judge. Luther's conscience was indeed transformed after he grasped the free grace of God, or as he puts it: "This straightway made me feel as though reborn and as though I had entered through open gates into Paradise itself."

The pastoral counselor may at any time be face to face with a tormented soul like Luther, someone who is trying so desperately hard to be justified before the God of justice—to find freedom from guilt—but has no peace for all of his or her extraordinary efforts. Such people may be some of those who truly impress others in the church with their noticeable piety and commitment. Yet their consciences, hidden from public scrutiny, remain unclean.

The Biblical Concept of Conscience

In the less detailed revelation of the Old Testament, there is very little about the conscience. By the time of the New Testament, however, there were more questions circulating in the Greco-Roman world about the way the human heart interprets and guides actions. The Greek word translated "conscience" in the New Testament is *syneidesis*, coming from two words, "to know" and "together." Literally the word means "the self that knows the self," or, as we might say, "self-awareness." It usually referred to moral awareness. The Stoic philosopher Epictetus defined conscience with a metaphor of pedagogy:

> When we were children our parents handed us over to a nursery slave who should watch over us everywhere lest harm befall us. But when we were grown up, God hands us over to the conscience implanted in us, to protect us. Let us not in any way despise its protection for should we do so we shall be both ill-pleasing to God and have our own conscience as an enemy.

The apostle Paul relates conscience to the concept of objective standards of right and wrong:

> Indeed, when Gentiles, who do not have the law, do by nature things required by the law, they are a law for themselves, even though they do not have the law, since they show that the requirements of the law are *written on their hearts*, their consciences also bearing witness, and their thoughts now *accusing*, now even *defending* them. (Rom. 2:14–15)

Even those who do not have the law of Moses still show moral sensitivity—they have conscience—and thus we know that the reality of God, including his goodness and power, are known instinctually and innately.

We cannot, of course, isolate the conscience in the human being like some kind of an intangible organ, or a spirit that inhabits the human soul. There are many theories of biblical anthropology that divide the human creature into a dichotomy of soul/spirit and body, or a trichotomy of soul, spirit, and body, but the Bible does not offer a compartmentalized picture of who we are. The rich biblical language of human nature—spirit, soul, mind, heart, will, inner being, and conscience—depicts the way our intangible selves, our spiritual selves, function.

To have a troubled conscience, then, means simply to be in spiritual conflict—that unsettled feeling of discord or dissonance in the soul that signals something is wrong. Shame is another way of describing that conflict. A person with an active conscience, one who is morally sensitive, is constantly comparing, as it were, a picture of the way things are supposed to be with the way things are. If the two pictures do not match, the conscience is troubled.

Fred kisses his wife good-bye before walking out the door to go to work, but the pain of the argument the night before leaves him with an unshakable discomfort inside that distracts him all day. He reviews a file from a business transaction two years ago, and gets a sick feeling as he recalls the cheating he did to get that deal through. He ends his day with a sense of failure because he has not been producing for six months now, and wonders whether others in the office look at him as a failure. It has been one more day when the conscience has seemed like an enemy, and Fred thinks of ways he can distract himself from its nagging stabs.

How Reliable Is the Conscience?

When people say, "Let your conscience be your guide," they are revealing a dependence on the inner voice of moral sensitivity. Indeed, we would be mere animals without such a capability. The shame of the troubled conscience shows the unique capability of human beings to be creatures of morality and value. If this inner voice says "ought not" it is because there is a wonderful principle of "ought" that only spiritual creatures can appreciate.

The Christian view of human nature, however, holds that there is no function in man that is unaffected by sin. One may follow one's conscience, but that does not mean that the conscience is an infallible guide to right and wrong. To put it another way, *the experience of shame itself (or lack thereof) does not always reflect reality to us.* When the apostle Paul dealt with the controversy surrounding meat offered to idols, he spoke of those who had a "weak conscience." The common practice in cities like Corinth and Rome was to take the meat of an animal used in a sacrifice in the pagan temples and sell it through the local market. Some Christians were jittery at the prospect of serving up (or being served) meat that had been bought at the local market but previously had been used in a pagan religious rite. Paul himself thought there was no problem with eating the meat: "the earth is the Lord's, and everything in it" (1 Cor. 10:26). But he appeals for tolerance for those with a "weak conscience" on the issue. We might say they had an underdeveloped or flawed ability to sense moral shame, and so they reacted out of imposed shame. They sensed guilt where there was none.

And so, at any time, a pastor may hear: "I feel so guilty for taking the antidepressants my doctor prescribed," or "I'm not sure I should go to my husband's company Christmas party," or "How do I deal with some of the music my teenager is listening to?" In the twentieth century we do not debate about meat offered to idols, but there are a multitude of other issues where Christians are trying to discern the boundaries of being in the world but not of it. There is no substitute for a trained, mature conscience.

We are all familiar with people who by any objective standard are living sincere and faithful Christian lives, but are hounded by a constant sense of condemnation. Like the young Luther, they are forever monitoring their beliefs and actions because of the sense of foreboding denunciation from God. Such an experience has been called many things, sometimes quite unhelpfully: lack of faith, poor self-esteem, compulsive personality. It is, however, essentially an issue of shame, the condition of a conscience that is chronically irritated and inflamed. The apostle John recognized this when he said that believers should know the right thing, try to do the right thing ("love not with words or tongues but with actions"), and then "we set our hearts at rest in his presence *whenever our hearts condemn us*. For God is greater than our hearts" (1 John 3:18–22).

Paul recognized both the value and the fallibility of the conscience when he examined his own actions in the face of considerable criticism by others.

> I care very little if I am judged by you or by any human court; indeed, I do not even judge myself. My *conscience is clear, but that does not make me innocent.* It is the Lord who judges me. Therefore judge nothing before the appointed time; wait till the Lord comes. He will bring to light what is hidden in darkness and will expose the motives of men's hearts. At that time each will receive his praise from God. (1 Cor. 4:2–5)

These comments have tremendous implications for the issues of guilt and shame. Notice the points Paul makes: (1) we will be judged by others (prompting either moral shame or imposed shame); (2) the judgments of others may or may not be right; (3) we should be careful even of our judgments about ourselves; (4) we should strive for a clear conscience; (5) however, the subjective state of having an untroubled conscience is not the same thing as the objective state of being innocent; (6) God is the only ultimate judge of our actions; (7) in this life we may not know with complete certainty whether a particular act was the right thing or not; (8) someday we will know where we did right and where we did wrong. These are verses worth pondering.

The logical question that follows from all of this is: if I can't trust my conscience, how am I going to discern what I should or should not do? Take away my conscience, and what am I left with? We should note that Paul does not say the conscience is *usually* untrustworthy, or that it should be ignored. We must pay attention to our consciences. But because consciences are not fixed, infallible guides, they need to be carefully trained and shaped. In other words, the ability to sense moral shame because of real guilt, and the ability to recognize imposed shame as a foreign intrusion need constant revision in our experience. Psalm 119 is a marvelous description of a man of God who knew what it meant to have a troubled conscience, who longed for a clean conscience, and who knew that he needed to understand the nuances of shame (see Table 4.1).

Table 4.1
Dealing with a Troubled Conscience

Text (Psalm 119)	Principle
Oh, that my ways were steadfast in obeying your decrees! Then I would not be put to shame when I consider all your commands. (vv. 5–6)	doing the right thing results in not having to have moral shame
I will praise you with an upright heart as I learn your righteous laws. (v. 7)	the conscience is a learner
I have hidden your word in my heart that I might not sin against you. (v. 11)	truth needs to be assimilated into one's innermost being
I have set my heart on your laws. I hold fast to your statutes, O Lord; do not let me be put to shame. I run in the path of your commands, for you have set my heart free. (vv. 30–32)	freedom from shame comes from following God's paths
Give me understanding, and I will keep your law and obey it with all my heart. (v. 34)	a healthy conscience is a trained conscience
I will speak of your statutes before kings and will not be put to shame, for I delight in your commands because I love them. (vv. 46–47)	the conscience must face the challenge of discerning between what is shameful to others, and what is right
Though the arrogant have smeared me with lies, I keep your precepts with all my heart. Their hearts are callous and unfeeling, but I delight in your law. (vv. 69–70)	those whose consciences are hardened may be those who falsely accuse and impose shame
Your word is a lamp to my feet and a light for my path. (v. 105)	the conscience's tutor is the Word of God

Text (Psalm 119)	Principle
I have strayed like a lost sheep. Seek your servant, for I have not forgotten your commands. (v. 176)	we must not forget that we are constitutionally limited and fallible (natural shame), and need to be sought out by God

Because our consciences need to be trained and developed continually the pastoral counselor can be glad for the many facets of pastoral care that can in different ways acheive that goal. Several sessions of pastoral counseling hardly provide the opportunity for the shaping and nurturing of a conscience. Forms of ministry like preaching and teaching and small groups or other forms of accountability provide the consistent influence of truth and grace that can tutor this tutor we call conscience.

The Hardened Conscience

Salvation is a process whereby troubled consciences come to a place of peace because of the reconciling work of God. If human beings were uncomplicated, that would mean that whenever they actually transgressed, there would be a sense of moral shame that would drive them to repentance, confession, and the cleansing of conscience. Despite the fact that we often meet people at this level, and that it is a real privilege to lead someone to the forgiving grace of God, we often deal with those whose consciences are troubled when they do not need to be, or whose consciences are dulled and ineffective when they should be screaming alarm.

The latter kind of person is what the psalmist meant when he spoke of "arrogant" people whose "hearts are callous and unfeeling" (Ps. 119:70). Jesus looked at the many people who would not hear his message and said, "this people's heart has become calloused; they hardly hear with their ears, and they have closed their eyes" (Matt. 13:15). So too Paul referred to "hypocritical liars, whose consciences have been seared as with a hot iron" (1 Tim. 4:2). We immediately know what they are talking about.

A young man comes to the pastor embarrassed and demoralized after finding out that after only a year of marriage, his wife has gotten into an affair with one of their best friends. He found out not by a confession on her part, but through rumor. Worst of all, she is showing no remorse about it. When the pastor contacts her, he is surprised at how coolly she explains that she has needs, and that her husband has ignored them from the start. She simply dropped from sight in the church a month earlier when the revelations came, and she is already making plans to move in with the other man. Her friends in the church have vastly different ways of sizing up the situation: she has just backslidden temporarily says the optimist; another wonders how committed she ever was to her husband or to God; still another says that no one should be surprised, after all, *anyone* married to *that* man would go looking for greener grass. But who really knows what is going on in her conscience?

What can the pastoral counselor do when the husband comes in looking for help? There is, of course, no reason why a pastor cannot or should not try to make contact with someone who is reportedly acting wantonly. The pastor should show an open door to someone who has real spiritual needs. A call or a note in the mail can provide that open door.

When dealing with someone whose heart really has turned hard, however, the pastoral counselor may have no opportunity for direct contact. If then it is an injured party with whom the pastor does have contact, the issue at hand may very well be how to cope with the fact that we are often powerless to change the destructive behaviors of others. The victim may be looking for something that he or she can do to soften the hard heart of the other, but may need pastoral advice on the order of Romans 1:24–28. God gives these people over to what they choose to do. Freedom is an awesome privilege—and dangerous.

The experience of moral shame is a God-given warning function of the heart, but it is possible for human beings to feel the warning and yet ignore it. Some doctors smoke, some lawyers break the law, and some pastors flirt with moral sin. Such are the ironies of human behavior. What is the road that leads someone to a hardened heart? There probably was a time when the pain of conscience poked at the person's heart. But there was something more compelling, some desire that won out over conscience. Over time, the pain of conscience became less and less noticeable. There was a chorus of other inner voices rationalizing or minimizing the sin. In the end even those voices died down because the conscience had been reduced to a faint whisper, not hard at all to ignore. The heart became hard, the callous complete, the searing finished. Finally, it became even easier for other desires to have an easy passage with the conscience conveniently crusted over.

Jesus gave the bare truth: there are some who are hardened toward God and others, and they never will turn. And yet the Scriptures also hold out the possibility that the person who appears to us most calloused of heart may be spiritually slain by a conscience activated by God. Like a fissure in the earth releasing the pressure of subterranean forces, something breaks through.

What is the role of the pastoral counselor in such situations? There are several key scriptural principles that need to be held in balance:

- No person is beyond redemption, and thus it is worth appealing to even the most haughty person.
- We have no absolute way of knowing whether the person is sensing moral shame, even if he or she does not admit it.
- The moral decisions of another person are not in our control; the spouse or friend, no matter how much they want to, cannot turn a magic key and produce the right spiritual attitude.
- Prayer for the convicting work of the Holy Spirit is always appropriate (John 16:8–11).
- Those who have to live with or around the calloused person cannot compromise their own values to adapt to the digressions of the shameless person. Scripture says that there is a fundamental conflict between light and darkness, righteousness and unrighteousness (2 Cor. 6:14–15).

The Cross, Salvation, and Guilt and Shame

If guilt and shame are obvious universal human predicaments (and secular psychology has only further confirmed their universality), then the pastoral counselor has the unique privilege of offering the only comprehensive solution to all manifestations of guilt and shame. To put it in a nutshell, *the Christian gospel offers forgiveness for guilt, cleansing of conscience for moral shame, vin-*

dication for imposed shame, and God's acceptance in the face of natural shame. This message of salvation in the broad sense is further validated by the Christian view of sin, which is the only realistic way of sizing up who we are, where we are responsible, and where the faults of others lie as well. Because there is an antidote—a complete and effective antidote—it is not unbearable to look at the problems in us and others.

Here pastoral counseling and other forms of ministry like proclamation come together. The same message of the cross preached in the pulpit is the gospel presented in pastoral counseling—in a particular, personal way—to individuals struggling with guilt and shame.

Salvation and Guilt

When someone seeks pastoral counseling because of "guilt feelings" one of the most crucial issues to sort out is the objectivity of guilt. As long as we think of guilt merely in subjective terms we will at best be trying to alleviate symptoms without applying a cure. All too often the people who are dealing with imposed shame go needlessly rummaging around for the key fault in them that has caused displeasure in others, while those who have a load of moral shame may be more inclined to look at their unsettled feelings instead of the root causes. The logical progression from good diagnosis to proper treatment to final cure must be held intact in pastoral counseling. Real, objective guilt must be identified and owned.

Because we live in an age of moral relativism the pastoral counselor will occasionally be talking to someone who has no concept of the objectivity of guilt. It would be nice to be able to repair houses rather than foundations, but sometimes pastoral counselors have no choice in the matter. Analogies to civil law may help to explain, but if the person has no respect for that either, it may be very difficult to get across the concept of real guilt. Here is where the pastoral counselor will need to recall that it is ultimately the Holy Spirit who will "convict the world of guilt in regard to sin and righteousness and judgment" (John 16:8).

At the core of the Christian gospel is the conviction that in Christ God has provided forgiveness from guilt. The proclamation of this truth is as incisive in counseling as it is in preaching. Forgiveness is what makes a qualitative difference in family, friendship, and church.

"In those days, at that time . . . search will be made for Israel's guilt, but there will be none . . . for I will forgive the remnant I spare" said the Lord through Jeremiah (50:20). Guilt nullified. Debt settled. This is not Christian cliché. It is a theology that must be crystal clear in the mind of the pastoral counselor, because it is only as we communicate the objective issue of guilt that we can hope to address the subjective experience of shame. Because Jesus was "full of grace and truth" he reveals both the devastation of our sin and the restoration offered through the God of grace. Because his death was an atonement, guilt can be alleviated through confession and faith rather than punishment.

Salvation and Moral Shame

In an ideal situation, those who really are guilty of something come with a sense of moral shame to speak with a friend or pastor. They come with a soiled conscience wanting to be purified, or, as it says in Hebrews, "let us draw near to God with a sincere heart in full assurance of faith, having our hearts sprinkled to cleanse us from a *guilty conscience*" (10:22). Whereas the Old Testament sacrificial system was unable "to clear the conscience of the worshiper," the blood of Christ will "cleanse our consciences from acts that lead to death, so that we may serve the living God" (9:9, 14).

The critical step in seeking release from moral shame is confession. Psalm 32:5 says: "Then I acknowledged my sin to you and did not cover up my iniquity. I said, 'I will confess my transgressions to the Lord'—and you *forgave the guilt* of my sin." When the pastoral counselor witnesses someone uncovering his or her guilt, there are so many questions that come to mind: *Does this person fully understand what he or she has done? Is the degree of remorse appropriate to the level of sin? What is the motive behind this confession? Would this person display the same regret to the person he or she sinned against as to me? Does this person properly see his or her responsibility? Will this person feel the same way tomorrow?*

There is that all-important moment when the person tells "the story." It is a sensitive moment, a time when the pastoral counselor must not get in the way with premature observations or judgments. The pastoral counselor will seek to draw out what is going on the heart of the person confessing personal guilt. On the other hand, we cannot expect perfect perception of the state of the person's heart. Like so many other learning experiences in life, coming to grips with personal culpability often comes both in a moment of realization, and as an ongoing process of learning.

One of the best biblical examples of someone processing his guilt and shame is the case of David's prayer of confession after his sin with Bathsheba found in Psalm 51. The catalyst for his moral shame had been the confrontational "pastoral counseling" of the prophet Nathan. The discomfort of David's heart is shown when he says, "my sin is always before me," "let me hear joy and gladness; let the bones you have crushed rejoice" (vv. 3, 8), and begs for God's cleansing (v. 7). One of the most important indicators that David had grasped the cosmic significance of his culpability is his statement "against you, you only, have I sinned and done what is evil in your sight" (v. 4). Yet David still had more to learn. He was able to say both "I know my transgressions, and my sin is always before me" (v. 3) and "create in me a pure heart, O God, and renew a steadfast spirit within me" (v. 10). He knew, but he needed to know more.

Most important is that David knew that his God, because he was a God of salvation, could be approached for forgiveness from guilt and relief from the crushing impact of severe moral shame. Contrast this with contemporary society in which we pretend that sin is an anachronistic concept, shame is a neurotic condition, God is basically apathetic, and forgiveness is relatively unnecessary. It is an across-the-board lessening of the intensity of the most basic structures of reality, a reduction of life to mediocrity and banality. David knew the depth of his sin because he did not stifle his experience of moral shame. All that led him to the fullness of the salvation of God found in his forgiveness.

Salvation and Imposed Shame

We sometimes forget that the full biblical concept of salvation—
yasha in the Old Testament or *soteria* in the New Testament—is
rescue or deliverance from our enemies. We are saved from ourselves in that God helps us overcome the mastery of sin and its
penalty, but salvation is also a process of being delivered from external enemies. The work of Satan and the mischief of human enemies so often is the lie of false accusation. The word "devil" trans-
lates *diabolos* in Greek, which means "slanderer" or "accuser."
Satan, who is "the father of lies", uses imposed shame to inflict
harm. It should come as no surprise that we meet so many people
who have been beaten down and bruised with the blunt instrument
of false accusation, imposed shame.

The same gospel of Christ that offers us deliverance from our
guilt also proclaims that God does vindicate, and that he will reverse
the effects of every false, destructive accusation. There are no guar-
antees that we will not be victims in this life, but the Scriptures
invite us to a confidence based on the righteous judgment of God.
When those who manipulate through shame try to shrink other
human beings, to bend their heads down in shame, the truth and
judgment of God are the strongest allies of the victims. God will
bring to light what is truly right and truly wrong.

When the pastoral counselor discerns that he or she is talking
to someone who clearly has been wronged, there is an important
opportunity for comfort through validation. The Scriptures frequently provide assurance through the promise of God's ultimate
judgment and vindication. Some people can be so terribly confused
by the imposers of shame that it may not cross their minds until
they hear it from a pastor that what is being done to them is wrong.
The wife who really believes she is the cause of her husband's unem-
ployment (because he told her so) or the child who believes that
he is the cause of his parents' problems (because they told him so)
are the all-too-common instances of moral confusion that can result
from the smoke screen of imposed shame.

Paul and Peter both knew what it was to be accused of being
guilty for something that, in fact, was very good. The harassment
and persecution that Paul faced might have broken his spirit. His

enemies wanted his head bent in humility and shame, but instead he tells Timothy: "I am *not ashamed*, because I know whom I have believed, and am convinced that he is able to guard what I have entrusted to him for that day" (2 Tim. 1:12). Likewise Peter says that "if you suffer as a Christian, *do not be ashamed*, but praise God that you bear that name" (1 Pet. 4:16).

This too is part of salvation. We find in the Old Testament the often-repeated theme of the day of the Lord, which represented to the prophets and others who announced it a future time in which God would interrupt human history and do two things: judge and vindicate. Every act of false accusation (imposed shame) will be shown for what it is. Those who tried to throw guilt in the face of others will have it thrown back at them. The prospect of the day when the Lord vindicates himself and the victims of this world is meant to be a present-day encouragement that the imposers of shame will not ultimately get away with it.

Matthew applies to Jesus a text from Isaiah that juxtaposes two contrasting truths: the hard reality of God's judgment ("he will proclaim justice to the nations") and God's sensitive restoration ("a bruised reed he will not break, and a smoldering wick he will not snuff out") (Matt. 12:18, 20). These are words of great comfort. God's judgment is not a destructive tantrum, but a perfectly precise evaluation of who was really guilty and who was bruised or nearly broken by the careless acts of others. The day of the Lord is a time of compassion. There is salvation from imposed shame.

Salvation and Natural Shame

Natural shame is that experience in which we realize that as long as we live this life on earth, we are limited, fallible, and frail creatures. In what sense, then, can we say that salvation addresses the issue of natural shame?

There have been Christian theologies that view salvation as a state of perfection, even in this life. The emphasis is on the victory of Christ, not only in the work of the cross or in our final reunion with him, but in the here and now. It is a victory that eradicates sin and allows Christians to walk with upright heads not just because they are forgiven, but because they are perfect.

It is hard to reconcile such a claim with statements even from the likes of Paul who says he has not been made perfect (Phil. 3:12). There are numerous passages which encourage Christians not to give in to the temptations of the body or spirit, which label mistakes in attitude and action, which encourage a life of faithfulness and perseverance. Why would the Scriptures address, for believers, issues of greed, gluttony, gossip, immorality, theft, lovelessness, and a host of other issues, if they were not the kinds of mistakes that even believers can make? We are assured of the supernatural work of the Spirit reforming and reshaping our lives, while at the same time we live with a natural state of fallibility.

When the Scriptures encourage us to be humble (Prov. 15:33; 18:12; Zeph. 2:3; Col. 3:12; Titus 3:2; 1 Pet. 5:5), they are instructing us to remember that in this life, at any moment, on any day, we may stumble. We often get less done than we set out to do because we overestimate our abilities and resources. The Christian parent who does not assume that someday, for some reason, he or she will have to apologize to his or her child is not accepting the natural limitations we live with in this life. "Pride goes before destruction, a haughty spirit before a fall" (Prov. 16:18) because if our heads are generally cocked too high in the air, we are sure to step in a rut or trip over a stone (cf. Prov. 11:2, "When pride comes, then comes disgrace, but with humility comes wisdom"). The humility of natural shame is the best way to avoid the pitfalls of overestimating one's abilities or virtue or resources. Paul prescribed exactly this when he said, "in humility consider others better than yourselves" (Phil. 2:3).

Natural shame is something helpful and realistic. It is not to be discarded. Yet salvation does address this experience as well. When God says, "I will accept you," he is extending his saving hand to a creature who is fallen, and who (although renewed and restored in sanctification) remains a member of a fallen race. We are not saved because we are perfect or even because we are made perfect, but we are saved in spite of being imperfect. This is one of the most basic elements of biblical theology, and yet it is so often ignored or misapplied in the way Christians think and act. There are two great perversions of the principle of the saving grace of God: one says that grace is conditional upon merit (an exaggerated natural shame that says, "God will accept you when you measure up") and another says that grace has provided complete victory in this life (an eradication of natural shame through triumphalism).

The pastoral counselor bears a great responsibility in that his or her attitude toward the counselee can have a profound influence. If we can know that God accepts us in spite of our shortcomings, then the counselee needs to see that message modeled in the counselor. People need to know that they can discuss their faults and failures, and still be accepted.

The impact of one's theological understanding of sin, guilt, shame, grace, and salvation on the counsel one gives is enormous. There is no substitute for a clearly understood, biblically balanced theology that sees the value of moral shame, the crime of imposed shame, and the careful equilibrium of confidence and humility in a healthy sense of natural shame.

The Cross of Christ—The Focus of Shame

If there is a last word to be given about guilt, shame, and salvation, it issues from that cosmic intersection of human need and divine assistance: the cross of Christ. There is one overwhelming, compelling reason to believe that God has decisively dealt with sin and guilt, and will deal with the shameless perpetrators of human pain: God himself stood in the spot of the greatest shame ever experienced in the universe, and in so doing, began the work of unraveling the guilt and the shame that has beset the human race since Adam and Eve.

We observe three ways in which guilt and shame were central to the drama of the crucifixion of the Son of God: (1) Christ took the punishment appropriate for the guilt of humanity, so that human beings would not have to take it themselves; (2) he experienced what was inherently foreign to him: the moral shame of humanity; and (3) the ridicule, derision, and rejection that his crucifixion represented was the ugliest moment of imposed shame ever perpetrated in history. Indeed, Christ came specifically for this purpose: to pay for the guilt and to nullify the shame that in every generation has pushed people far from God.

One of the primary functions of counseling is to bring about the application of the saving sacrifice of Christ in the lives of counselees. Look at the cross of Christ, and you cannot make guilt a superficial issue; you cannot doubt that God knows the struggles of the conscience-stricken soul; and you cannot say that God has no idea what it is to be ridiculed or belittled.

The pastoral counselor will do well to keep in mind one pivotal biblical text that ought to be brought up in any counseling session dealing with guilt or shame. In it we have biblical revelation coming full circle, from innocence to shame to the reconstruction of broken humanity:

> Let us fix our eyes on Jesus, the author and perfecter of our faith, who for the joy set before him endured the cross, *scorning its shame*, and sat down at the right hand of the throne of God. Consider him who endured such opposition from sinful men, so that you will not grow weary and lose heart. (Heb. 12:2–3)

The "joy set before him" was the vision that Jesus had of guilt-ridden people cleansed. He saw to the other side of forgiveness, and so he "endured the cross." It was worth the pain. By an act of love greater than the world has ever seen or would ever see, he was willing to be seen as the incarnation of guilt itself (cf. 2 Cor. 5:21). He was willing to be accused, convicted, humiliated, and put to shame so that we could gain freedom from it. The pain and humiliation of the cross meant less to Christ than getting us past our guilt and shame and being restored to him.

How did Jesus scorn the shame of the cross? By triumphing over it. Granted, this is the experience of the unique Son of God, but at the same time it is the path that was blazed for us by a kind of pioneer. He put shame in its place. He let us know that while shame has been central to the human story, it would not have to be its concluding chapter. Moral shame is only a passageway to confession and forgiveness, and imposed shame is only the sting of the lies and deceptions of others. If truth is an eternal principle that God enforces, then the pain of imposed shame will inevitably fade before God's righteous gaze.

Perhaps one of the greatest challenges of the pastoral counselor is to bring into contact people's everyday problems with these eternal principles. While it is obviously naive (and compassionless) to think that we can throw a few biblical passages at people and solve their problems with guilt and shame, we would be equally mistaken to think that the kinds of biblical truths discussed in this chapter are merely footnotes of our counsel.

Because guilt and shame are such fundamental spiritual issues, people who come to a pastoral counselor wanting to talk about them often realize they need spiritual answers. They want to feel right before God and before others. They may be very confused about whether they are guilty or not, or why they have had experiences of shame. They may not even use guilt or shame as the label for the stresses or turmoil they are experiencing. But ask the right questions: Do you feel like you're hiding who you really are? Do you feel like nothing you do is ever good enough? Do you sense a distance between you and God or others? Often we find one more son or daughter of Adam shuddering and hiding in the trees.

4

Shame's Impact

The emotion of shame is a powerful force in our lives and is central in governing or modulating our behavior. When we feel shame, we are inhibited, shut down, turned inward. Like the bit and bridle that a small rider can use to control a mighty horse, shame functions to shape our thoughts, feelings, behaviors, and relationships through its inhibitory function. This chapter will consider four concerns often encountered by pastoral counselors and common to the human experience in light of the important role shame has in our daily living.

These four concerns—identity and self-esteem, intimacy and relationships, addictions and other problems in living, and, knowing God—are central to living as God has called us to live. Jesus summed up all the commandments, all the guidelines for living, in the following words: "'Love the Lord your God with all your heart and with all your soul and with all your mind.' This is the first and greatest commandment. And the second is like it: 'Love your neighbor as yourself'" (Matt. 22:37–38). Guilt involves unloving acts (transgressions); shame blocks the giving and receiving of love.

105

Resolving our guilt and shame is at the heart of loving God, loving others, and loving ourselves.

Identity and Self-Esteem

Our culture has sometimes depicted the attainment of self-esteem as the highest goal. Magazines address self-esteem on their covers, many books and seminars promise to raise self-esteem, and various movements promise to clarify our identity. The perfect body, more money, a new car, the right relationship, or achievements are all depicted as the way to self-acceptance. Advertisers tempt and manipulate the masses with the promise of feeling good if only their product is purchased. We are left with the illusion that if we perform well enough, then we will be loveable, free from the pain that comes with negative or low self-esteem.

Despite so much effort and attention given to raising self-esteem, our culture is composed of people who actually do not like themselves and are confused about their identity. Many of us do not know who we are but know we do not like what we do know. Our attempts at being thin enough, powerful enough, or good enough to be loved have failed. So many have so much, have accomplished so much, and yet are desperately dissatisfied with who they are.

The Christian gospel says much about self-esteem but in a different context than our culture offers. Our call to love God fully and love ourselves as we love others is a radical departure from what surrounds us. Rather than doing, performing, or obtaining, we are to love. Rather than competing in our attempts to be good enough by being better than others, we are to find our value in relationship to God and to others.

Understanding how a person's self-image develops will enable the pastor to have increased empathy for those who have low self-esteem. Parishioners with low self-esteem, or those who are unrealistically negative in their self-evaluation, have learned to judge or evaluate themselves in this manner. Empathetic responses such as reflective listening communicate care and understanding to counselees and help them learn to be more realistic about their true identity.

A person's identity, the definition of "who I am," develops out of relationships. As Adam knew who he was by his relationship with the Father, we initially learn our identity and self-worth in the primary relationships with our parents. Self-esteem—the value or worth placed on the self and our emotional reactions to our identity—is continually clarified in relationships. Most significantly, we can come to understand our identity and self-worth in a manner similar to Adam as we relate to our heavenly Father.

Children are born with an innate need to connect with others and without a sense of their own uniqueness. Anything that they can sense (hear, see, touch, smell, taste) is experienced as a part of themselves. Thus, children's experiences of themselves are dependent upon the treatment they receive from their parents. Children who are cared for and who experience their parents responding to their unique needs with clear and consistent boundaries develop a sense of acceptability or goodness about themselves. Such children have experienced the parents as a mirror in which the parents' treatment of them is a reflection of their identity and worth. As these children mature, they develop a cognitive and emotional capacity to experience themselves as unique and separate from their parents.

During early childhood, the child imitates the parents' care, often using a teddy bear or other object as a soothing substitute for the parents. A child may be overheard talking to himself as if the parent were talking to him or may, in play, treat an object as he is treated by his parents. As the developmental process continues, the child separates further from the parents, acknowledging that his or her thoughts and feelings are different from those of the parents and that "you are you and I am me." At this point, the child has internalized the parents' care and can provide self-care and make moral decisions without the parents' presence. The child now develops many relationships outside of the family, drawing close to others while still maintaining a clear sense of his own identity and worth. The child's connection with the parents and their reflection of the real nature of the child facilitated the development of self-esteem, leading to positive connection with others.

Often the effects of sin in our world result in problems in the parent-child connection. When parents do not adequately or consistently connect, for whatever reason, the child experiences disconnection and the emotion of shame. The disconnection may be due to the presence of alcoholism or abuse in the family. However, disconnection is not limited to these extremes but occurs wherever there is disconnection, such as unavailability of the parents due to other demands, their own emotional difficulties, or a lack of understanding or recognition of the needs of the child. Imposed shame is then bound or paired with the corresponding needs, thoughts, feelings, and events, further inhibiting the person.

During disconnection, the child will attempt to establish a reconnection to meet his innate need and experience relief from the pain of imposed shame. The child does not know how to care for himself; rather, he follows the pattern of how he was treated by his parents. If the parents did not respond to a need or called the child "stupid," the child treats himself in like manner. Or, if the parent was ineffective in connecting with the child by neglecting to meet the needs of the child, the child will imitate the parent's neglectful behavior. In such situations, the child may either deny needs and focus on caring for the parent or ignore the needs of others and seemingly care only about himself. The need for connection is so strong, the parent so valued, that the child keeps thinking of the parent as "good" for it is the parent who defines reality for the child. As the child develops, he experiences great distress at attempting to separate from the parent for to do so would leave him in a state of being "bad." He senses he can have relief of the pain of shame only if he connects with the parents.

As such individuals reach adulthood, much of their identity is bound with shame. They desire to connect with someone who will care for them and relieve the pain of the shame. However, as the parents are experienced as good and adult children are disconnected from parents, these adults are left in a state of being "bad" or having low self-esteem. Their relationships with others are characterized by trying to come too close (overdependence) or of being unable to connect (contradependence). Unable to connect, they are unable to separate from the parents and they live to either please or resist their parents. Reflecting off mirrors of disconnection, such people experience themselves as unlovable, bad, and unworthy.

Attempts to reconnect through performance, pleasing the parents, or achievement are inadequate. A child, no matter what the age, is unable to make the parent connect. The adult child has internalized the mirrors of the parents and continues to reflect to himself a distorted image of his identity, hidden in the imposed shame of disconnection. To obtain self-esteem, the shame must be resolved and the person needs to acquire accurate mirrors off which to reflect the true self.

The true self, a self that may be esteemed, is revealed as the shame is resolved. Ultimately, self-esteem is not a goal but a consequence of shame resolution. When people strive for self-esteem, they often experience an increased awareness of their own inadequacy, their own failure to "be good enough," and a heightened awareness of their disconnection. Attempts at increasing positive self-statements, weight loss, winning more, or other attempts at self-esteem enhancement provide only momentary relief from the pain of low self-esteem. It is only through the resolution of shame that the self can be realistically esteemed.

Resolution of each type of shame results in a capacity to love ourselves and to love others. Moral shame resolution facilitates personal responsibility and an appropriate sense of pride. By testing our own actions and not comparing ourselves with others, we can take pride in ourselves (Gal. 6:4). This healthy and realistic pride acknowledges our strengths and weaknesses and dependence on God. Facing and accepting our guilt, requesting forgiveness, and receiving and applying forgiveness to ourselves clarifies our uniqueness, worth, and autonomy. To avoid resolving moral shame requires denial or hiding and implies a belief of either inadequacy or a lack of worth of the self. As each person is worthy, the pain and shame involved in resolving guilt are secondary to the redemption and freedom available for the person.

Imposed shame is like a blanket that covers true identity. People left in disconnection often feel bound up and will strive to deny who they are in attempts to reconnect. They have lost touch with their value and their personal power. Furthermore, their failure to hold other people responsible for disconnection distorts their perception of the identity of other people as well. The confusion regarding responsibility unrealistically devalues the self and over-values the other. An accurate attribution of responsibility and then resolution of the shame creates the opportunity to love the other in the same manner that I would love myself.

Acceptance and resolution of natural shame produce an awareness of need and dependence on God. We are not fully self-suffi-cient. Embracing our natural shame is necessary before we can accept the reality of our human experience. Identifying and accept-ing our place in reality may wash away the imposed shame that has been attached to our needs. The necessary reconnection is with our Creator, our heavenly Father. We can mirror off the Father, seeing who we are as we look to God and treat ourselves as God has treated us, imitating his treatment of us. As we respond to the love of God, we are then able to love God and to love ourselves and others in the same manner. The self-esteem problem is no longer a focus. Rather, shame resolution results in reconnections, realistic self-awareness, and freedom from the inhibitions that have distorted identity and blocked the receiving and giving of love.

Intimacy and Relationships

We relate to others in the manner that we relate to ourselves, for to love your neighbor as yourself is to love yourself as you love your neighbor. Thus, our self-esteem, our relationship with our-selves, and our relationships with others are interrelated. Our innate need to connect with God, with others, and with ourselves drives us toward relationships while our experience of the emo-tion of shame inhibits us, prompting us to hide and withdraw.

Relationships are the fundamental experience of being human. Our very survival and the development of the identity and self are dependent upon relationships. Our deep need for connection leaves us vulnerable to the pain of disconnection. Shame functions to pro-vide protection from the consequences of and limit the exposure to disconnection. Thus, relating involves balancing the need to con-nect with the desire to avoid shame feelings. We must be vulnera-ble to connect, or relate, yet we need to protect ourselves from the pain of being too vulnerable.

The resolution of moral and imposed shame assists us in balancing our competing needs for connection and protection. Shame identifies our limits or boundaries. People are designed to use shame as a positive regulator of their behavior and to feel shame when they have transgressed or have become too vulnerable for the situation. At such times, we are motivated either to correct the wrong or to avoid the vulnerability. The shame experience may lead people not to cheat on their taxes or to be careful with whom they share personal information. In contrast, the narcissistic or selfish person as well as the self-less, self-contemptuous person lacks a healthy shame response.

The appropriate response to our natural and moral shame is the realistic awareness and acceptance of ourselves. The self can then be shared with others and others can be loved and accepted. Accurate attribution of responsibility for disconnection or transgressions allows for rapid reconnection and release from shame. Such attribution of responsibility facilitates clear ego-boundaries and thus increased safety in revealing the self and receiving from another person. Such revealing and accepting is the basis for knowing another person. *Intimacy, then, requires the active and consistent resolution of our shame. As we only connect at points of vulnerability, it is necessary that we learn to be vulnerable. Vulnerability becomes safe only as shame is resolved.*

The reciprocal nature of relationships is revealed in Jesus' words that we are to "love our neighbor as ourselves." We can accept the inadequacies of others as our own shame is resolved. The release of unrealistic demands and expectations on the self produces increased freedom in extending grace to others. In a similar manner, treating others with grace increases the likelihood that grace will be applied to the self and that the other will respond with grace. As we reveal ourselves to others or are vulnerable to them, it is more likely they will share themselves with us.

It is often revealing one's self to another that results in the pain of imposed shame. Openly seeking connection leaves one vulnerable to the pain of disconnection. In many situations a pattern has developed in which attempts to be connected predictably result in disconnection. The adult who strives to win the approval of a parent yet receives only the parent's disapproval or lack of interest will predictably experience disconnection and imposed shame. The pain of the imposed shame can be avoided by changing expectations, by decreasing vulnerability in the situation, and by developing a new relationship with the parent based on the reality of the parent's predictable response patterns. In this manner, resolving the imposed shame leads to an acceptance of parents as they really are and thus a more intimate (albeit less ideal) relationship.

Resolving imposed shame may result in sadness as one accepts the reality of the other person. Just as young children mentally and emotionally maintain their image of their parents as "good," adults often hold unrealistic hopes for and expectations of others. Resolving the imposed shame holds reality up to the fantasy, often initially resulting in a painful sadness followed by freedom. The sadness continues the need to release the unrealistic expectations and hopes, which allows the freedom to live in the truth. *The acceptance and resolution of all types of shame allow for the real awareness and acceptance of our boundaries and provides protection from excessive vulnerability.*

Addictions and Other Problems in Living

There are significant consequences to the failure to resolve shame. In addition to low self-esteem and relational difficulties, addictions and other psychological problems may be caused or intensified by unresolved shame. Many if not most of the life problems that individuals disclose to the pastoral counselor somehow involve unresolved shame and guilt. Problems in living are often avoidance, escape, or sedation of the pain of shame.

Addictions and other compulsive behavior patterns function in this manner. For many, prior life circumstances have resulted in a pairing, or shame bind, of many needs and emotional reactions with shame such that when the need or emotion occurs, they feel shame. For example, many have experienced disconnection when they have been angry and thus have an anger-shame bind. When they perceive that something is wrong or they have been wronged, they feel shame rather than anger. Their anger is blocked; no change occurs. Thus, their anger is not resolved, and they just feel shame.

The anguish many feel from shame is a powerful motivator to find relief, but when reconnection is not readily available, they seek a form of sedation or escape. Almost any activity or object can be used to provide sedation or escape. There has been a rapid increase in awareness during the last few years of the addictions to alcohol, illicit and prescription drugs, relationships, eating, sex, and spending or shopping. These activities or objects are used to provide an escape from or sedation of the shame.

If the use of these activities or objects results in reconnection with others or self, thus leading to resolution of the shame, the use of the activities or objects will be minimal or cease altogether. In such a case, there is no addictive process. However, these activities and objects rarely address the cause of the disconnection and hence are ineffective in reconnection. Nevertheless, some brief relief from the painful emotional experience of shame is experienced and it becomes more likely that the process will be repeated. If the intensity of the shame is great or the coping resources of the person are low, the use of these activities or objects will increase rapidly. Human beings develop addictive processes to objects or activities that provide only partial relief from the pain of the shame or offer an illusion of reconnection.

The consequences of these activities and objects often contribute to further disconnection and, in many cases, guilt. Both imposed and moral shame are thus likely to increase in intensity. *A cycle develops in which one feels shame, engages in an addictive or compulsive act to obtain sedation or escape, experiences further shame, and again engages in the addictive or compulsive behavior.* An addiction is evident when the feared deprivation of the activity or act produces greater emotional pain than was originally present. In addition, psychological sedation is, in many ways, analogous to physiological drug habituation in that both require greater amounts to provide the same effect over time. The addiction-shame cycle leaves a person feeling trapped, humiliated, helpless, and wanting more.

People who use alcohol for sedation and then become dependent experience episodic relief from their pain yet in disinhibited and sedated states engage in behaviors that are destructive to themselves and others. In addition, the alcohol is destructive to the body.

Denial is often evident as such people are driven to avoid the pain and shame, which intensifies their perceived need for more alcohol. They seem blind to the consequences of their addiction to themselves and others. Likewise, the man who feels inadequate as a son, husband, and father may pour himself into his work, hoping that if he is successful he will feel some relief from the shame. The success he experiences in the workplace comes at the expense of being a son, husband, and father, which magnifies his sense of disconnection. Feeling more shame, he devotes greater time to work. The shame cycle is perpetuated.

Shame is a powerful force in many other problems in living. Depressive reactions may result from shame-emotion binds in which the resolution of emotional reactions such as anger, hurt, or sadness is inhibited. Phobias may develop as shame and fear are paired. The phobia serves as a defense to avoid the object or event paired with shame.

Eating disorders also manifest shame binds. Overeating is fueled by the pain of feeling empty inside, hungry to feel connected, craving to be loved, cared for, and respected. Consuming food provides temporary gratification and pleasure, a respite from the pain of shame. However, a judgment against the self often follows and the shame cycle continues. Other eating disorders involve the displacement of the shame away from the self and onto food. Bulimia, a pattern of binging on great quantities of food followed by purging of the food by vomiting or other means, functions to modulate the shame experience. The bulimic individual experiences a constant state of shame and feels helpless to change. Binging produces change by intensifying the shame experience; the purging then provides an eruption of the emotion, bathing the person in shame. Just as a good cry allows many to let go of tension, the purging of the food temporarily releases the feelings of shame. In a similar manner, many sexual dysfunctions involve shame paired with wants or needs as well as unresolved shame and guilt in the relationship.

Family violence also has its roots in unresolved shame. Physical abuse is rooted in the experience of powerlessness and shame. Often abusers were also victims of abuse and relive the humiliation and rage from both their historical perspective as well as the position of the parent. Their internal image of the abuse they received factors into the rage they displace on others and thus reproduces guilt and shame.

Sexual abuse survivors are left with intense imposed shame. The abuse activates experiences of powerlessness, violation, humiliation, and disconnection. Often, when confronted with such intense shame, individuals withdraw deep within themselves and disconnect from others in order to have a sense of protection. The contempt and disgust regarding the violation is then turned against the self as a means to release some of the pain of the shame and to keep alive the illusion that the perpetrator is good and that connection is possible. The separation of self may manifest itself on a continuum from self-contempt to multiple personalities. Perpetrators often attempt to force a reconnection through violation as a means of reducing the shame, anger, and powerlessness they experience. Perpetrators are most often themselves survivors of sexual abuse and are continuing an all-too-familiar cycle.

Each of these dysfunctional living patterns functions either to provide escape from or to sedate the pain of shame. The patterns are dysfunctional in that they do not address the need for reconnection. Rather, the escape or sedation only delays the shame experience and often produces more guilt, disconnection, and shame. The shame cycle not only increases in intensity in the individual but also within the family and then across generations. *If guilt and shame are not resolved, individuals and families experience continued disconnection, low self-esteem, relational difficulties, isolation, and the loss of love.*

Knowing God

Loving others and ourselves is dependent upon loving God: "We love because he first loved us" (1 John 4:19). God as the source of love has communicated his love for us in both word and deed. Yet many are unable to experience God's love and have great difficulty moving past an intellectual knowledge of God's characteristics. Such people can recite God's attributes but share in private moments that they feel far away from God, or that he seems harsh, judgmental, and unavailable. To such individuals, hearing about a loving, personal God only contributes to their experience of dis-connection and feelings of shame.

Difficulties in connection with God take many forms. For some, there is a sense of stagnation in which they have intellectual knowledge but little or no intimacy or emotional involvement. For others, God seems abstract, unreal, and uninvolved in their lives. Still others experience God as critical, judgmental, distant, and unavailable. Such people often believe God is involved with others but not with them. The pastoral counselor will frequently discover that such people have experienced a distant, neglectful, or abusive parent, most often a father. For many people, their view of and relationship with God are often indicative of their relationship with their own father or father figure. Frequently such people report feeling comfortable with a loving and kind Jesus but are fearful or angry with the idea of God the Father. All these examples identify an experience of disconnection from someone and a corresponding sense of disconnection from God.

Psychologists use the term "transference" to refer to the uncon-scious assignment or transfer of the attitudes and feelings origi-nally associated with one person who has been personally signifi-cant to another person. This process of responding in the present to a person as if the person were someone else is common and may be either positive or negative. During early development, children transfer their image of the parents and then their relationship with the parents to themselves. When the shame and guilt are actively resolved, the transfer tends to be positive and both the parent and child are esteemed. Children with such experiences are likely to develop a positive and realistic sense of God. When shame is not resolved and imposed shame becomes chronic, a negative trans-fer occurs and the child not only lacks self-esteem but is also likely to transfer the negative feelings and attitudes to God.

The transference regarding parents also impacts a person's rela-tionship with God. Children, no matter the age, are likely to expe-rience God in a manner similar to how they experienced their fathers. People whose fathers were involved, responsive, and con-nected tend to experience God in a similar manner. Others, who experienced their fathers as absent, neglectful, abusive, or other-wise disconnected, have great difficulty experiencing positive emotions regarding God. For these individuals God is only the distant, harsh, righteous judge. God's attributes of goodness, mercy, and love seem incongruent with their image of what a father is.

The imposed shame that results from parental disconnection functions like a wall between a person and God. Resolving moral shame is made more difficult as the conscience is overwhelmed with thoughts of guilt yet relatively void of feelings of acceptance or love. Thus, when such individuals experience moral shame they tend to hide from God and others or to confess excessively in an attempt to attain relief from the pain. Either strategy is insufficient to remove the weight of the imposed shame and the person feels removed from God, from others, and from themselves.

The pastoral counselor can assist such individuals in their pursuit of knowing God by aiding in the resolution of the imposed shame. The realistic attribution of responsibility for the experienced disconnection and any associated guilt is the beginning of clarifying the transference. Feelings and attitudes toward parents and others that have been too hard to acknowledge influence a person's capacity to give and receive love. The expression of such feelings and attitudes begins the process of being realistic in accepting and loving self and others. Anger or fear that is related to a parent can be attributed to the source of the emotional reaction and then resolved. Realistic attribution of the emotions and attitudes is necessary to separate these experiences from God. God can then be known for who he is and not as a reflection of the parents or other people.

Resolving imposed shame and growing in a relationship with God ease the resolution of moral and natural shame. It is ironic that the acknowledgment of guilt often becomes more painful due to the awareness of God's holiness and the desire to honor God yet the experience of grace is deeper and the freedom in Christ richer in the experience of moral shame resolution. The meaning of forgiveness and the experience of being loved and forgiven are intensified as more of the self is shared with God and as forgiveness, grace, and love are accepted. Such love facilitates secure acceptance of God's provision for our inadequacy and our need for him. Natural shame is no longer dangerous or denied. Rather, accepting our inadequacy frees us to connect with God's sufficiency.

We can embrace our relational position as children of God. Our identity in Christ is experienced in our mirroring of our heavenly Father, seeing ourselves as God sees us. The pastoral counselor has much to offer those who struggle in loving God fully and loving others as they love themselves.

5

Counseling
Shame-filled People

The majority of those who seek pastoral counseling are experiencing life difficulties in which guilt and shame have a significant role. Some seek counseling fully aware of their guilt and desire relief from the painful shame that is its consequence. Others are unsure of their status and may be pursuing counsel to help clarify their concerns. Still others come with the burdensome pain of undeserved shame and an accompanying harsh, critical, and unrealistic self-evaluation. They feel unlovable and unworthy. Each phase of the pastoral counseling process presents challenges. This chapter will consider some of the frequent issues encountered when working with people who have unresolved shame and guilt. In the remaining chapters, a case study is offered, which illustrates the use of this counseling model.

Encounter Stage

Establishing a counseling relationship may be difficult for the person experiencing intense shame. Frequently, people are unsure what their problem is; they only know that they feel bad. While their words may express confusion, their body language often communicates shame. Poor or no eye contact, looking away from the pastor when speaking, and lowering the head are all signs of the experience of shame.

Three verbal styles may inform the pastor that the counselee is experiencing shame. Individuals who express self-condemnation or self-doubt or who belittle themselves are often experiencing shame. The self-appraisal of such individuals tends to be unrealistically harsh. A second verbal pattern is evident when the counselee appears to be defensive, apologizing for taking the pastor's time, expressing no needs or vulnerability, or significantly minimizing hurt, anger, fear, or pain. In this situation, the shame may be bound with these emotions, prompting suppression. A third situation involves those who are focused on their works and performance, often demanding perfection of themselves or others. The pastor can mentally note these styles in the process of attaining a pastoral diagnosis.

Dependence issues are often evident early in the first interview. Individuals who are hounded by imposed shame often experience either overdependence or contradependence. Overdependent people underestimate their ability to cope and experience a strong desire to be connected with another person. The pastor can assist such people in identifying and owning their own thoughts and feelings and attributing positive change in their lives to their own actions.

In contrast, contradependent people deny their need for others and appear to be self-sufficient. The pastoral counselor may respond by helping these people identify and own their thoughts and feelings as well. In this case, thoughts and feelings involving inadequacy, need, or vulnerability can be identified and owned. In doing so, the shame bound with these thoughts and feelings can be weakened. Both dependency styles involve difficulties with boundaries.

The establishment of clear boundaries at the beginning of the counseling process and the maintenance of these boundaries throughout counseling are essential to addressing the needs of the parishioner. These boundaries include a clear definition of the purpose of meeting, the allotted time for each session and the total number of sessions anticipated, the responsibilities of each party involved, and an arrangement for any communication outside of a session. Since imposed shame occurs through the violation of boundaries, the establishing of clear boundaries is essential in trying to resolve imposed shame.

The "diagnosis" by the pastoral counselor involves both the problem the counselee presents as well as factors that contribute to the problem that become apparent during the counseling. When unresolved shame has been identified as a problem, the pastor may assume that the counselee is motivated to obtain reconnection in order to resolve the shame. Several questions arise. With whom is the person attempting to reconnect? Whom does the counselee feel ashamed in front of? Who is responsible for the disconnection? Is there unresolved guilt?

Unacknowledged or Unresolved Guilt

Some individuals seek pastoral counseling either to determine if they have guilt regarding a situation or to attempt to justify a pattern of behavior in which they sense guilt but do not want to change or discontinue their behavior. The person who is troubled by thoughts and is confused as to whether the thoughts are wrong, the man who is having an adulterous relationship and attempts to rationalize his behavior, or the woman who has decided to have an abortion and wants to know she will be forgiven are seeking some reassurance and relief from the pastor. The challenge for the pastor is to understand and relate to both the objective truth and the subjective emotional and mental experiences of these individuals.

It is significant that a person would seek a pastor to explore such concerns. Almost anyone knows that it is not hard to find someone who will approve of your actions, especially in a relativistic society. That a pastor was chosen suggests that the parishioner has placed some value on the authority of the pastor's response. The pastor is in a position to offer far more than definition of guilt or confrontation of the guilty.

Principles for determining guilt or innocence are found throughout Scripture. The process of assigning moral culpability was discussed in Chapter 2. The story of Jesus with the woman at the well illustrates for us that specific guilt is in the context of a unique person's life and needs. The pastor can offer understanding, a reflection of God's love, and a bridge for reconnection with the heavenly Father. The identification of guilt leads to an awareness of our vulnerability, of our need for God.

Engagement Stage

As counselees attempt to resolve their problems, they seek to understand what they are experiencing, why it has happened, and what they can do about it now. The pastor can offer understanding at many levels. Many counselees experience considerable relief as they learn to identify and own their personal experiences. Teaching and then assisting a counselee to distinguish between guilt and shame often produce significant change and hope. Furthermore, when guilt and shame have been identified and differentiated, more specific plans can be made for change.

The inhibitory effects of shame are often evident as counselees seem unable to identify what they feel or think. The presence of the emotion of shame inhibits the awareness of other emotional reactions and decreases the ability to be creative, think abstractly, or solve problems. Furthermore, shame prompts social withdrawal or isolation and decreases risk taking, which inhibits change. The pastor may observe that the counselee "doesn't get it" or seems to be "frozen."

At such times, the pastoral counselor may identify for the person that the emotion of shame appears to be interfering with the ability to understand. Counselees may be asked what emotions they feel in addition to the shame or "behind the shame." The pastor may direct them back to an awareness of the disconnection, using the counselee's thinking abilities to identify the nature of their feelings. Or the pastor may assign a writing exercise to be completed between sessions. Such exercises can be designed to assist counselees in identifying their thoughts and feelings in a specific situation, track their thoughts and feelings across time, identify scriptural truths or promises and link them to their experience, or link their thoughts with their feelings.

People feeling shame are often inhibited in their capacity to receive acceptance from others. The pastoral counselor may provide encouragement, support, and counter the inhibitory effects of shame by encouraging counselees to expose the shame and corresponding thoughts. A phrase such as "shame loses its power as it is taken out of hiding" can offer support and direction as well as become a tool parishioners use when they are not in a session.

At times, strong transference develops in which the counselee projects onto the pastoral counselor attributes of those who imposed shame. The person may experience the pastoral counselor "as if" the pastor was uncaring, the pastor's boundaries were unfair, or other similar responses that are actually relevant to the earlier imposer. In addition, the pastor can often conclude that if the transference has occurred in this relationship it is likely that it has occurred in other relationships. The pastor can identify these and offer an interpretation to such counselees, which may help them accept and clarify their own thoughts and feelings.

In order to identify transference, the pastoral counselor must be aware of his or her own reaction to the counselee. For some pastors the overdependent or contradependent person evokes a strong reaction. Some common reactions include the desire to have a person feel better or to take care of him or her. For others, a power struggle may develop in which the pastor feels attacked by the counselee's projections or senses a threat to his or her own boundaries. The counselee may experience an intense desire to be deeply connected with the pastor, sensing that such a connection could be the reconnection that would resolve shame. The seemingly always needy counselee may elicit a sense of inadequacy or failure within the pastor, evoking the pastor's own shame response. Or, such behavior may evoke anger in the pastor as he or she senses that the incessant demands are too much. In some situations, pastoral counselors may encounter a power struggle in which they sense a need to justify and defend their own boundaries. In other situations, the unique circumstance regarding the counselee's shame, such as having been abused as a child, evoke strong reactions within the pastoral counselor.

The pastor needs to both identify and respond to countertransference. It is highly advisable that all pastoral counselors have collegial or supervisory relationships in which they can process concerns of the counselee, the process of the counseling, and their own countertransference. In some situations, the pastor can resolve the countertransference by acknowledging its existence and sensing the acceptance of peers. In other cases, it may be helpful for the pastor to share his or her reaction with the counselee for the counselee's benefit, as a means of clarifying boundaries and simultaneously demonstrating the humanity and vulnerability of the pastor. If the pastor has had this reaction, it is likely others have had similar reactions and this may contribute to the difficulties the counselee experiences. In yet other circumstances, it may be best to refer the individual to another pastoral counselor—particularly if the content of the counselee's shame evokes very strong reactions within the pastor and the pastor is responding to his or her own reactions rather than to the counselee.

As the emotion of shame prompts hiding and social withdrawal, the pastoral counselor does well to link the counselee with others in the church or community. Such efforts are often resisted but, with encouragement and support, counselees can experience relationships with the opportunity for reconnection and shame resolution. Sunday school classes, small groups, or support groups may all present opportunities for social connection.

Disengagement Stage

Shame prompts people to attribute positive change to forces outside themselves and to have difficulty accepting that their actions were influential in the new feelings, thoughts, and behaviors. Commonly, the counselee attributes the change to either the pastor or to a miraculous act of God. While there is truth in this, it is important for counselees to accept that their efforts and the risk they took have contributed to the changes they have experienced. It is important that counselees accept that they can take actions that will make a difference in their lives and experience. The helplessness often experienced by those feeling shame can be counteracted by the pastor's attention being directed toward what they have done that resulted in change.

In some circumstances, exposing the shame results in suppressed processes, such as depression. For example, consider people who were sexually abused but have attempted to ignore or minimize the memories and have experienced a chronic state of self-contempt and shame. As they become aware that they are feeling shame, the feelings that have been suppressed by the shame may become evident. At such times, these people may be highly vulnerable to depression and may actually seem, for a time, to be doing worse. Referral to a trusted mental health professional would be in order and would benefit the counselee.

Short-term Strategic Pastoral Counseling is designed to clarify the boundaries and minimize excessive dependence on the pastor. Yet dependency issues will continue to be evident for many at the conclusion of the counseling. In addition to recognizing and affirming the counselee's role in the change process and facilitating connection with and support from other people, the pastor may need to reinforce the boundaries at the end or following the conclusion of counseling. Such maintenance of the boundaries may be paired with suggestion for actions that would direct counselees to appropriate and functional means of having their needs met.

People who struggle with unresolved guilt and shame present unique challenges to the pastoral counselor. While inhibited by shame, such people are also ripe for significant change. Their request for pastoral counseling represents a major step in breaking the chains of guilt and shame that have encumbered them. The pastoral counselor, sometimes a guide, other times a fellow-traveler, can provide an opportunity to be heard and understood, and an opportunity for reconnection.

6

Session 1:
The Encounter Stage

Pastoral counselors encounter shame and guilt in virtually all counseling situations. The consequences of the fall and the resulting sin nature in human beings account for the distress and problems in life we all experience. Guilt and shame are the central human problems; other problems are outgrowths of these issues. The pastoral counselor is particularly qualified to provide understanding, insight, and guidance regarding these key issues. While guilt and shame are always relevant issues in understanding a problem, the role each has varies greatly from one situation to the next. At times, an identifiable sin is clearly the cause of the distress and the guilt must be addressed to resolve the problem. In other situations there is no specific sin for which the counselee is responsible yet he or she experiences a sense of shame. In these situations the resolution of imposed or natural shame is the focus of the counseling. In yet other situations natural shame, or the plight of the human condition, is the distressing factor. A hypothetical case study is here offered that outlines common issues encountered in Strategic Pastoral Counseling.

Susan, a thirty-seven-year-old woman who had contacted her pastor first by a note and then by phone, sat anxiously in his office. "I feel so embarrassed to be taking your time like this." Susan nervously glanced around the pastor's study, amazed that this room that she had seen so many times before now looked so different. It was the perspective that made it different. She had never sat in the chair across from his desk as one of those people from the congregation who had come in for pastoral counseling. Her role for years had been that of the model leader, a Christian education coordinator who was the best a pastor could ever hope to find. To sit in the seat of the givers was one thing; to be a receiver, quite another.

Pastor Newquist was not a bit surprised at her reticence. "No need to feel embarrassed. I'm happy to try to help in whatever way I can." He could tell when she called the previous week that she had something important to talk about. In fact, he was greatly relieved at her request to come and talk because he had sensed for months now that something wasn't right. He had asked her numerous times how she was doing but she always claimed that everything was okay. Even when she called, she couldn't come right out and ask for help, but only hinted that maybe there was something spiritual that she needed some advice about. She finally made the appointment, assuring Joe Newquist that whatever it was, she was sure there was some simple explanation.

Commentary: As is often common in pastoral counseling, the pastor knew many things about the person requesting counseling. The existing relationship provides both advantages and disadvantages in that opinions and some background information are already available to each person in the counseling relationship. Entering a counseling situation does change a relationship, as Susan quickly noticed. The pastor, noticing her discomfort, provided a sense of safety by reflecting back her expressed feelings of embarrassment and providing some reassurance. Susan displayed a shame-need bind as she revealed that she had hidden her needs by telling others she was "okay" and by minimizing her needs during the phone call. Her relationships had been characterized by her defense against shame. She lacked peers because she had been a helper but had a hard time receiving. It is not uncommon for those who appear to have it all together and give so much to others to be driven by the pain of shame.

Susan continued. "I don't know why I feel so . . . unsettled, I guess you'd call it, these days. I have a good marriage, we have three wonderful kids—did you know that Joanie has gotten the lead part in the high school musical? In fact, I don't know how anyone could ask for better kids. I have had wonderful opportunities in my life. I was able to get my real estate license three years ago. I've done so many different things in this church. And now, to be able to be a leader in the CE ministry, well, that's something I've always wanted to do."

"Could you expand a bit on what you mean by 'feeling unsettled'?" interjected the pastor.

Commentary: The pastor attempted to help Susan focus since her experience of shame inhibited her ability to define her problem and express her needs. As she defended from shame by recounting all the reasons she might be worthy (and yet acknowledged these are not enough), he directed her back to her need and, in doing so, gave her permission to be vulnerable. His open acknowledgment of her expressed emotional reactions increased her perceived safety to share further.

"Oh, I don't know if that is even the best word for it. It's so hard to describe. Maybe it's all in my imagination. My husband thinks it's just menopause. Maybe he's right."

"Is that what you think?" As Joe Newquist looked at her, it struck him how fragile her smile was beginning to look. Now that he thought about it, for months or even longer there was something incongruous about how she presented herself. Almost too smiley, too pleasant. The tenser the situation, whether it be a contentious CE committee meeting or her dealing with a disgruntled parent, the more "proper" and pleasant her demeanor. It made Joe recall that such people even made him second guess himself. *If the people I am serving can keep their irritations and anger to themselves, why can't I? I wonder if some think of me as a hothead leader?*

Commentary: Susan appeared to have responded to her anger, which had shame paired with it, by trying to be "extra good." Psychologists refer to this as reaction formation, the unconscious use of reactions opposite of real but unacceptable feelings. Joe was perceptive in observing her anger. His previous relationship with Susan assisted him in identifying her needs. In addition, Joe's personal shame was activated by what Susan presented. It is very common that pastoral counselors will feel their own shame as they work with others. The intensity of the counseling relationship will evoke the counselor's personal issues as well as address the needs of the counselee. It is critical that counselors be aware of their own shame issues. Joe did not address his personal reactions with Susan— which is appropriate. Rather, he might make a note of the issue and, if needed, explore it later with a colleague, supervisor, or trusted friend.

"I'll tell you what I think." Susan paused for a long time, looking like she could burst into tears any moment. "I think there must be some sin in my life that God is punishing me for. I've thought about it day after day. Believe me, since I made this appointment with you, I've really been seeking the Lord on this."

"Why do you think the problem is some specific sin?" There was another long pause.

"Because I feel so guilty." She pronounced the word "guilty" as if it were something caught in her throat that she was practically gagging on.

Commentary: People develop an explanation for their feelings, thoughts, and behaviors. A common reaction to feelings of shame is to assume personal guilt. Susan confused shame with guilt. The pastor chose not to correct her at this time but rather used her words as he listened and thus built trust, connection, and safety.

"Is that feeling of guilt attached to anything in particular?"

"That's part of the problem. It just kind of floats around. It seems like these days there is hardly anything that I *don't* feel guilty about. One day it's seeing my mother in the nursing home and feeling like we should never have put her there." Susan paused, choking back her emotion. "The next, it's that I should have been friendlier to the clerk in the grocery store." It appeared as though these words were as difficult to get out as the previous. "It's stupid stuff—really stupid stuff."

"When else do you feel so guilty?"

Here was a very long pause. It seemed like five minutes to Joe, but it was probably barely a minute. Joe decided not to jump in and take her off the hook. Susan allowed a few tears to surface, and then wiped them off quickly. "I feel like a fake in church. I have to admit that when I see you glance at me, I practically get a knot in my stomach because I can't help but think that if you really knew me, you wouldn't want me in the church. And to a degree I feel the same way about lots of different people. If they only knew . . . "

Commentary: Susan acknowledged that she felt as if she had a false public self that was acceptable to others and that her real self would be unlovable and unworthy. Many individuals who experience chronic imposed shame describe such a false self in which they hide their needs, vulnerability, and emotions. As Susan experienced, such individuals frequently feel disgust and contempt toward the false self yet greatly fear revealing the true self. Susan's affect-shame bind was activated as she prevented herself from crying or even revealing her tears.

"Knew what?"

"The one thing I keep coming back to . . . "Joe noticed how Susan paused here, looking directly at his expression as if to see if it was safe to go on. "The only thing I can figure out is the fact that Frank and I *had* to get married." Now Susan stopped, deliberately studying the pastor's expression at this crucial juncture.

"I didn't know that. What makes you think that is what is burdening you now? What has it been, sixteen, seventeen years?"

"Seventeen. It's the only thing I can think of."

"Do you frequently think about it?"

"Not really. As a matter of fact, I've only been thinking about it recently because I had this appointment to see you and I didn't want to come in as a blank slate."

Joe noticed that though Susan had told him something that was not easy to say, there was no sign of relief at having said it. "Tell me, seventeen years ago, were you able to confide in anybody?"

"As a matter of fact, Frank and I talked to the pastor we had then right away."

"What happened?"

"He was just great. He helped us work through it, and helped us have a normal kind of wedding."

"What did that mean for you—to work through it?"

"Oh, a lot of things. I felt so ashamed before God, and had to admit to God that I was wrong and accept his forgiveness. It took me even longer to forgive myself and to forgive Frank."

Commentary: Susan again attempted to justify her feelings of shame by finding some personal guilt. Concluding that she was feeling shame related to the pregnancy and wedding, Joe began to identify the type of shame. He observed that she spoke relatively freely and with little emotion, suggesting that this might not be her central distressing concern. As she had already identified a personal transgression, he assessed if and how she had resolved the guilt and moral shame, the question in the back of his mind being whether or not she had ever repented. Clarifying that this had occurred and recognizing that she continued to feel shame many years later, Joe began to broaden the question. Susan's nonverbal communication suggested both her experience of shame and her need to connect with him at that moment in order for her to be able to continue. His responses to the content of her speech as well as to her behavior were empathetic displays of his respect for her and built trust and connection.

"What about other people?"

"The only other people who knew were our parents. Frank's parents were okay about it, I guess. We never really knew. And mine . . . " Susan immediately choked up and again quickly wiped away the tears. When she was able to speak there was an almost child-like quality in the way she spoke. "Mine couldn't handle it."

It was obvious Susan was having a hard time going on. Joe asked, "What do you mean 'they couldn't handle it'?"

Commentary: Joe observed and responded to Susan's nonverbal communication, which suggested both her experience of shame and her need to connect with him at that moment in order for her to be able to continue. Her suppressed emotional expression associated with speaking of her parents suggested to him that this topic was very important and needed to be explored further. He again used her words to encourage her to continue telling her story and to facilitate her experience of connection. At this point, a pastoral counselor who was not aware of the different forms of shame could have stumbled, producing further disconnection and thus additional shame for Susan. Had Joe assumed that there was this one simple key, the moral shame of unresolved guilt, he might have had her doubt that she had been forgiven of the sin after her first confession and encouraged her to repeat the confession process. When this would have failed to provide relief, as she was already forgiven, Susan would likely have felt more shame. As Joe was to discover, the disconnection responsible for this shame was due to the behavior of others.

"My father never said a word about it to Frank and me after we told him. He usually let Mom do the speaking, but we always knew that he gave her an earful behind the scenes. Things were definitely different from that time on. I always assumed he was ashamed of me, but sometimes he almost acted afraid of me."

"What about your mother?"

Susan's expression turned flat, even cold. "She had a lot to say. Mostly going over all the things she had taught me. I-told-you-so kind of stuff. She was angry for a long time. People at the wedding probably thought I was the typical happy bride, but there was little joy inside. I know that she and my dad talked a lot about what this would mean in the church. She even thought Frank and I were foolish for wanting to reveal our secret to the pastor. I almost think that she would have preferred that we kept it a secret from her."

Commentary: Susan's shame regarding this incident was now identifiable as imposed shame added to moral shame. The imposed shame was due to the disconnection she experienced from her parents. In this situation, the disconnection occurred by their neglect or ignoring of her needs, feelings, and repentance. Rather, her mother's focus was on how the wedding and pregnancy would affect her and not Susan.

Joe inquired, "What happened after the wedding?"

"We went on our merry way, had our first child. No big deal. We were just one more happy Christian family. But every now and then, usually when I was having some kind of conflict with my mother, she would mention my 'stumbling.' It was kind of her way of putting me in my place, I guess. It worked, anyway."

"How did it 'work'?"

"It just shut me up. What could I say?"

"Apart from the issue of your having been pregnant when you got married, was this kind of tension with your mother typical?"

Susan nodded deeply. "Oh yes. She always knew what to say to get us kids to conform. She knew what strings to pull. Except with my older brother. He just kind of checked out of the family when he left the house. He couldn't take it . . . " Susan stopped abruptly and her demeanor changed from rigid to nervous again. "I shouldn't really be talking like this about my family. You're probably thinking I'm blaming them—which I don't. They meant well, I know."

Commentary: Susan revealed that she had long been motivated to attempt to release her feelings of shame by connecting with her mother through pleasing her. She described the use of imposed shame as a means of control, in this case her mother attempting to control Susan. Imposed shame had kept Susan enmeshed with her mother. Susan had experienced a distortion in her identity, feeling small and defenseless in her mother's presence. Her implied anger toward her mother for this treatment was inhibited by the shame she felt. In addition, she confused blaming and intent with assignment of responsibility, further magnifying her experience of imposed shame.

Joe sensed that an opaque curtain was coming down on the issue of Susan and her parents. He decided to turn the discussion back to its starting point.

"I'd like to come back to what you first said, and try to understand a little more what is actually going on right now. You first described it as feeling 'unsettled.' What does that mean, really? In what aspects of your life do you feel unsettled?"

Commentary: The pastor sensed her defensiveness and is respecting Susan's reluctance to further explore the issues involving her parents. He clarified the boundaries by refocusing on the salient issue, her feeling "unsettled." In doing such, he would gain further knowledge as well as help her better understand her own experience by putting it into words and sharing it with someone else. Joe made a note regarding the historical factors related to her imposed shame as well as her reluctance to explore this.

Susan seemed a little more comfortable with the shift of topics. She thought for a moment before answering. "It seems to be a general kind of thing. Like I'm off-balance. I've always prided myself on how many plates I could keep spinning at one time. But lately I feel like they're all about to fall to the ground at once. My friends and family have always marveled at how I could raise three kids, have a career as a teacher and then start another as a realtor, and be one of the most visible leaders in the church. I suppose I almost overdid it sometimes. I don't know, it's all so confusing. I always thought I was serving God with all my mind, heart, soul and strength, but inside sometimes I almost resent it all, resent him."

Commentary: Susan defended against her feelings of imposed shame by striving for perfection, which was a way of demonstrating that she was good enough for reconnection. The disconnection she experienced from her parents became linked to her relationship with God—a common experience. She had transferred onto God the expectations and responses of her parents. Unable to be secure in her connection with her parents, she was insecure in feeling loved and accepted by God. At this point in the interview, she felt safe and accepted as she revealed her pain, frustration, and resentment. Joe, sensing her vulnerability, continued by challenging her to question her understanding of connecting with God.

"What you're saying doesn't surprise me. Tell me, can you think of two or three people in the church whom you admire because they do seem to love God with all their heart, mind, soul, and strength?" asked the pastor.

"Yes, there are two that come to mind right away."

"Are these people who razzle-dazzle people with how many plates they are spinning?"

"No, actually they're not razzle-dazzle people at all."

"Do you think, Susan, that perhaps it's time to start over with a new understanding of what it means to please God?" At this Susan could only nod while weeping openly.

After a couple of minutes Susan collected herself and Joe continued. "Let me ask you a couple of important questions so I can better understand how to help. Have you been having bouts of depression or hopelessness? Have your sleeping or eating patterns changed during this time?"

"No, not really. I guess I have spells where I'm down, but they usually pass."

"Just keep in mind that if this ever becomes the case, it would be important for you to be seen by a psychologist or psychiatrist to see if you should be treated. You understand that as your pastor, I am happy to give you pastoral counsel, but if things get severe, you may need something beyond what I am able to provide."

Commentary: The pastor assessed the severity of Susan's experience with a focus on common symptoms of depression. While pastoral counselors are not mental health therapists, it is important that they be knowledgeable about the symptoms of major disorders. A person who regularly feels much imposed shame can experience clinical depression, which may include suicidal thoughts. Joe further defined the boundaries in terms of what he could offer and when a referral would be appropriate. It is important to note that a referral to a psychologist or psychiatrist would not necessarily preclude his continued work with Susan since pastoral counseling would address some needs that would be ignored by others.

Susan now seemed much more at ease and attentive to what the pastor had to say. He continued. "Let me tell you just a few thoughts off the top of my head. First of all, it sounds like you came through a very trying and complicated time seventeen years ago. It's complicated because it involved you and Frank, your interaction with God at the time, and then your relationship with your parents and even with others who didn't know your 'secret.' You had a real issue of guilt to deal with at the time, but you were also dealing with being pushed and pulled in your social relationships at the same time. Second, it sounds like you were repentant at the time. You confessed and got counsel from your pastor, and yet you say it still bothers you a great deal today and is even interfering with your life in general. That leads me to my last observation. You seem to be looking for a 'key' to explain the distress you're going through. You say that the only thing you can think of is this sin from the past. That sin may or may not be the central issue. If I were to take a guess, I'd say that your 'unsettled' feelings relate to much broader issues in your life. That's what we'll have to explore. Whatever the case, I think that the issues of guilt and shame seem to be central for you right now, and I think we should talk about that. Let me ask you a few questions."

To every question Joe put to Susan she nodded with no hesitation. Do you think people would reject you if they really know what kind of person you were? Do you very often feel like hiding, like crawling into a hole? Do you feel like your emotions are often numb or painful? Do you question your leading in the CE area or even being a member of the church? Do you sometimes feel like a failure in the other roles you play in your life—wife, mother, real estate agent? Do you sometimes feel distant from God?

Joe told Susan that he wanted to present her with some ideas about guilt and shame, that she would work on applying these principles to her own situation, and that they would get together again to discuss what she came up with. Joe used a one-page handout to go through definitions and descriptions of guilt, and the three forms of shame (see Appendix and Chapter 2). Susan agreed with Joe that the concept of guilt as an objective issue of innocence or lack of innocence was certainly something that society has tended to minimize. While she thought that the word "shame" was a very strong description, she readily identified with the experiences of moral shame and imposed shame as the pastor explained them. As Joe explained natural shame Susan seemed less attentive, and Joe assumed it was because she was captivated to the point of distraction by the idea of distinguishing real guilt and felt shame, either justified or unjustified.

Commentary: Joe began to teach Susan only after he had listened to her, used her own words to clarify her meaning, and helped her accept and define her own experience. Had he attempted to introduce teaching early in the session, he may have squelched her revelation, contributed to an experience of disconnection, and not have understood Susan's experience and needs. Susan now felt safe, understood, and connected. His teaching applied an understanding of guilt and the forms of shame to her unique experience. Joe thereby assisted her in applying abstract definitions to her personal experience. Recognizing the limits of what she could comprehend at the moment, he referred her to readings that would strengthen her understanding and contribute to an ownership and personalization of these understandings.

With no hesitation Susan set up an appointment in two weeks with Joe. He explained to her the parameters of his counseling her, particularly that as a pastor he had neither the training nor the time for ongoing therapy. Rather, he would meet with her at least a couple times again, but not more than five times. He told her he wanted her at this point to simply concentrate on understanding the concepts of guilt and shame, and then reflecting on her own situation, taking notes of any thoughts that developed. He gave her a small book that further explained the issues and told her he expected her to read it as soon as possible.

After Joe prayed for her, Susan left. He was confident they would have plenty to talk about when they next met.

Commentary: Joe concluded the session by further defining the boundaries of their counseling relationship. Boundary definition facilitates realistic expectations, further trust, and increased safety in the relationship. The boundaries included how often they would meet, the purpose of meeting, and what to do until their next session. The homework he recommended would further reinforce the teaching as well as assist Susan in accepting her experience and prepare her for the next session, thus maximizing her efforts. Furthermore, he provided hope and encouragement.

In this session Pastor Newquist successfully completed the encounter stage. A safe and accepting environment was provided and a counseling relationship was established. Boundaries were defined at both the beginning and end of the session. Susan's reason for scheduling the appointment, her state of "feeling so unsettled," was defined and clarified. In addition, relevant historical material was obtained. The pastoral diagnosis was developed and refined during the session. They identified imposed shame as a key issue and got some perspective on the moral shame Susan had experienced in the past. The pastor checked to make sure Susan was not exhibiting symptoms of serious depression, and ruled that out. They identified that her relationship with God had been affected by the imposed shame as she focused on her performance and strove for perfection. In addition, her relationships with others were also impaired as she had no peers. The session ended with mutual agreement on the goal of the counseling and with an assurance of hope.

7

Sessions 2, 3, and 4:
The Engagement Stage

The goal of the second stage of Strategic Pastoral Counseling, the engagement stage, is to explore the affective, cognitive, and behavioral aspects of the problems and identify the resources for coping or change (Benner 1992). Pastor Newquist, having successfully connected with Susan during the encounter stage, recognized that she had likely revealed only some of the aspects of her concerns. During the second session, he would assess her motivation by checking whether she completed her homework. He would further evaluate her capacity to respond to short-term pastoral counseling.

Session 2

"Well, how have you been doing since we talked two weeks ago?" asked Pastor Newquist. He was worried because if anything Susan appeared even more anxious than in the first meeting they had. When she hesitated in responding, he wondered if they were back to square one.

"Frankly, it's seemed like two months. So much seems to have happened. Not in my circumstances, but in my thinking. I guess I've got a lot of questions now that I didn't have before."

"Like what?"

"I'm not sure I know where to begin. I'm not even sure what I ought to ask. I'm afraid, you know, that some of my questions will displease God. I'm sure they do."

"Listen, Susan. I can assure you, God can handle your questions. He's big enough for that. And I guarantee that there is nothing that you've been wondering about that hasn't already been voiced in the Scriptures themselves. Just look sometimes at some of the questions asked of God in the Psalms or Job. Why don't you start with something that you've thought about more than once."

"Forgiveness," Susan blurted out. "I thought I understood forgiveness, but now I'm not so sure. I thought that I understood God's forgiveness of Frank and me for having to get married, but there have been times when I have felt as guilty as I did seventeen years ago. I thought that I was a forgiving wife, putting up with some of Frank's problems, shortcomings, you know, but I have to admit that we've had a lot of tension in our home for the past five or six years. And I think I haven't even entertained the notion of forgiving my mother. We just settled into a pattern of survival with each other for so many years." Joe Newquist noticed that Susan spoke freely now and seemed to have shed the anxiousness that showed in her face at the start.

Commentary: Susan's experience of shame began to diminish as she gradually exposed her shame, her inadequacies, and her needs. The pastor appropriately recognized that at this point, the content of what Susan would share was not as important as allowing her to begin sharing about her experience. Furthermore, he connected with her by providing both personal and scriptural assurance that her questions were permissible. By not reframing her need to ask questions as a faith or trust deficiency, he facilitated an increased trust and sense of safety in the counseling relationship and likely an increased openness to consider Scripture. The pastor noted that Susan spoke in a general way about "feeling guilty," indicating that she needed to further discern issues of guilt and shame. He recognized that Susan might be motivated to move to forgiveness before the wrongdoing was identified or the responsibility appropriately attributed. He noted her automatic response of "I'm guilty" and, in an attempt to discriminate between moral and imposed shame, encouraged her to further explore the issues. In addition, she appeared to be displaying a shame-anger bind that had contributed to her confusion regarding forgiveness.

Susan continued. "What we talked about two weeks ago was really helpful, don't misunderstand me. I guess I'm just trying to sort it all out."

"Why do you think forgiveness is an important issue for you right now?"

"It's the right thing, isn't it? I guess I realize that it's what I need, what I want to give. When we talked last time about guilt and shame, so much of it all seemed to apply to me." Susan paused as a sudden rush of emotion caused her to choke up. Joe noticed that as soon as tears came to her eyes she looked down in her lap and had a hard time looking at him. He remembered it had been the same in their first meeting.

"Well, that's something specific I wanted to ask you about today, Susan. I'm glad that you do see guilt and shame as issues that touch on your situation, because it certainly sounds that way to me. Could you give me some examples of where you see an application to you?"

Commentary: Pastor Newquist attempted to strengthen Susan's awareness and ownership of her shame feelings by directing her to provide personal examples. He had observed the physical signs of the shame experience and might have benefited from verbalizing these to Susan, noting the shame-affect bind. Each time she had a tear, shown anger, or expressed a need, she had a break in eye contact. She apologized, looked down, and manifested shame. Sharing with Susan these observations might have helped her identify them herself as well as deepened the connection she felt with the pastor, facilitating further shame resolution.

Susan reached in her purse for a folded-up piece of paper that Joe recognized as the handout he had given her in their first meeting. As she unfolded it he noticed that it looked like it had been handled quite a bit and had a lot of notes in the margins.

"Guilt," Susan started. "You said that guilt is the issue of whether a person has actually done something wrong or not. Right?"

"Just think in terms of a courtroom, Susan. We have courts so that we can objectively determine whether someone has done something wrong, against the law. We have to know whether people are guilty or not so we know how to react properly. So God has given us a kind of inner courtroom we call the conscience—though it has been known to make mistakes—and an external courtroom called the Word of God."

Commentary: The use of a metaphor to make an abstract concept understandable and applicable to daily living is often very effective. In addition, acknowledgment of the limits of the conscience is important in facilitating Susan's capacity to differentiate the various forms of shame.

"I do feel like I'm guilty. I feel it all the time. But isn't that what the Bible says about human beings? I know that it also talks about God's forgiveness, past, present, and future, but what about the 'deceitfulness of the heart' and 'our righteousness is like filthy rags'?"

"It's important to remember that guilt is not a feeling. More accurately, we should say, 'I feel ashamed,' or 'I think I'm guilty.' It's a mistake for us to think we are guilty of nothing, but also a mistake to think we are guilty of everything. Of course, the Bible does say we are sinners, that we are a guilty race, but it doesn't follow that we are morally culpable in every situation of stress or conflict in our lives. Justice requires that we weigh our actions in the balance and acknowledge true guilt, not less and not more. Tell me, as you thought about our discussion and read the book I gave you, how do you think shame applies to you?"

Commentary: Changing the use of language is important in changing thoughts, feelings, and behaviors. "Shame" is the best overall term for the felt emotion, whereas it is important to retain the objective sense of the word "guilt." This distinction is critical in resolving shame and guilt because only then can someone address guilt as a question of "have I actually done something wrong?" and the experience of shame as "why do I feel so disconnected?" The pastor alluded to the distinctions between natural and moral shame. He might have encouraged Susan to be more emotionally expressive, linking her feelings to this explanation.

Susan looked up and spoke calmly and deliberately. "It's me. That book described my whole life."

"For example?"

"Well, I guess that my big 'secret' would be an example of moral shame. That's pretty easy. It all gets a lot more complicated from there on. I feel ashamed around a lot of people. It's like I'm always afraid that they're going to find out what a big fake I am. I keep thinking, *if they only knew.*"

"Knew what?"

"Knew that I'm not really the person I present myself to be. I'm supposedly a leader in my work and here in the church, but I'm never satisfied with what I do and I feel like I keep running to the next thing so that people won't have time to see my shortcomings. Then I feel ashamed even in my own home. I go back and forth being angry with Frank for being the way he is and at the kids too, then feeling like I have no right to have any expectations of them. It seems like I'm a ping-pong ball going back and forth. And that very fact makes me feel like I've failed too. I mean, what kind of a wife and mother is that to be?"

"Sounds like a vicious cycle."

"You've got that right. It's just like a downward spiral, and what scares me is that lately I seem to have dipped lower than ever before."

"I can understand how that would scare you."

"It's not like I'm afraid I'm not going to make it, or something. I just want things to start moving in the right direction."

"Well, let's see what insights we can gain to help that along. What, after your reading, do you make of the concept of shame?"

"I'm not sure I understand it all, but I think it's what I've 'got'!" At this Susan smiled and seemed to relax more.

Commentary: Susan allowed herself to become emotionally vulnerable and the pastor might have been able to further connect with her and assist her in connecting with her own feelings and new understanding by addressing her emotional reaction. He might have said, "This is what shame feels like, how painful it is, how we feel like hiding. These feelings are real and may not necessarily tell you who actually is guilty but they do tell us we feel bad, disconnected." Through more empathetic responses he might have assisted her in decreasing her defensiveness through intellectualization.

"One important thing to remember is that we've all 'got it,'" said Joe. "In fact, we'd be in big trouble if we didn't have occasional experiences where we had that sense of inner conflict over something we've done. The other side of the coin is that it is possible for someone to have too much shame. When a person feels practically immobilized by shame, that's a problem that needs to be addressed. We need to stop and think where the shame is coming from. Is it the proper voice of a sensitive conscience, or is it coming from the expectations or perspectives others have of us? In other words, is the sense of disconnection due to something I have done or due to something someone else has done?"

"I know both kinds of experiences."

"That's good. Can you give me some for-instances?"

"I feel very ashamed when I 'lose it' around the kids or Frank. I never used to say things that I regretted later on. I surely never used names or swore." Joe could tell it was hard for Susan to talk about this.

"What kind of shame do you think that is?"

"Moral shame, for sure."

"How do you know?"

"Well, because it was my response to something I did that was wrong. I wish it was always that easy, though. There are plenty of times when I feel ashamed just because of who I am."

Commentary: The pastor took Susan through an example of moral shame. It would have been helpful for him to have summarized the example to strengthen Susan's understanding before moving into the next scenario about imposed shame.

"For instance?"

"I've never felt like I'm good enough around my mother."

Once Susan brought up the subject of her relationship with her mother it was like a floodgate opened. As she wiped tears from her eyes she randomly told stories of recent events and during her growing-up years in which her mother devalued her or belittled her. She alternated between rigid control and crying. Pastor Newquist let her tell her stories, and then suggested that here was a profound life experience in which some of her most basic attitudes about herself were being shaped. At this, she cried deeply for several moments as Joe sat quietly in order to show her support as she faced her pain.

When Susan asked Joe how she could get past her strong feelings about her mother because she really wanted to forgive and move on, they got into an extended discussion of what forgiveness would mean in this particular situation. Joe discussed the nature of imposed shame, helped her outline who was responsible, and helped her identify her anger. He reminded her that she could not forgive someone until she held that person responsible for the wrongdoing and that her anger was her response to identifying that her mother was responsible. Should she confront her mother? If so, when? Should she just try to "forgive and forget" it all and not say a word? Pastor Newquist discussed all the options with her so that she could see the implications of all courses of action, and then suggested she give it some careful thought and prayer.

Commentary: This discussion on the identification and resolution of imposed shame occurred in the context of Susan's expressed confusion and distress. Joe was appropriate in identifying that forgiveness in isolation would not solve her shame problem since she did not have a clear enough understanding of what transgression or act she would forgive her mother for. His discussion of attributing responsibility got the discussion past the simplistic thought of mere blaming as bad. He also made the very important, frequently misunderstood point that discerning her mother's responsibility did not mean that she was punishing her mother. Rather, the goal was to identify who was responsible so that the guilty party might be forgiven and the innocent party released of a false perception of guilt.

"There is one last thing," Susan said as the session was drawing to a close. "Frank is totally frustrated with me. He didn't understand anything of what I explained about our last discussion. I feel like our marriage is getting frayed to the point of breaking. He flies off the handle at the least little thing. What should I do about that?

"Any family is a complicated set of relationships, as you know, Susan. I wouldn't even venture a guess right now what might be going on with Frank in the midst of what you are going through. Would you like me to meet with the two of you when we next get together?"

"I think that would be a good thing."

As they set up a tentative time to meet in two weeks, Joe reminded Susan that their goal was to meet perhaps a few more times, but that it would not be ongoing. He told her he didn't want to speculate right now as to how Frank figured into the picture, or whether marital counseling would be called for. He obtained permission from Susan to share the content of their sessions with Frank and suggested that Susan ask her husband to read the book about guilt and shame. After Joe prayed for Susan, Frank, their kids, and her mother, Susan left.

Commentary: It is not uncommon for people to bring up very important material at the end of a session. Joe responded well to this by recognizing what Susan had shared and telling her that this concern would be addressed during the next session. To this end, he requested that her husband attend the session for the purpose of clarifying how the relational issues impacted Susan's experience of shame, and because he felt he had a pastoral duty to Frank as well.

Between sessions, Joe thought a great deal about his own responses of shame in different circumstances. He consulted with a colleague and reviewed both his boundaries with Susan in the counseling relationship and his own reactions to the content of the sessions.

Session 3

Joe Newquist was somewhat surprised that Frank was not hesitant about coming in to talk. He quickly found out why. Frank viewed this meeting as an opportunity to verify his complaints about his wife to a third party. Joe had run into plenty of other situations in which someone wanted to use the pastor as a kind of spiritual crowbar.

"I'm not sure how much more of this I can put up with," Frank said. "It's like living on a roller coaster. I told her she's probably going through her change. She didn't like that suggestion too much."

Commentary: As Joe listened, he became aware that Susan had minimized the depth of the problem in the marriage and observed Frank shaming Susan in front of him. Joe continued to observe the pattern between the husband and wife and did not intervene at this time so that he might understand the needs and reactions of each and so that he would be able to attempt to connect with Frank.

Joe could see Susan stiffen. "Could you describe for me some particulars?" Joe asked.

"Well . . . " Frank hesitated, as if it was hard for him to put his finger on what it was he was saying. "She blows up at me a lot more often than she used to. Then she usually ends up doing a lot of crying."

"What are the kinds of situations in which these blow-ups occur?"

Again, Frank hesitated. "It's usually over something stupid." Joe noticed that Susan alternated between looking resentful and defeated. "She never used to get so irritated when I'd have to work late—that would be one example—or we never used to fight over how to discipline the kids. Oh, we'd have disagreements, all right, but we used to be able to work it out without getting all upset. She never used to care if I had a drink or two after work, but now I feel like I've got to tiptoe around the house."

"What do you think has changed?" asked the pastor.

Both Frank and Susan hesitated, looking at each other as if to seek an answer in each other's faces. "We do love each other," Susan said. "I don't think that has changed." Frank nodded both at her and at the pastor. "It just seems like we're both on the edge of a cliff and it doesn't take much to push us over the edge."

Commentary: Susan expressed socially appropriate thoughts and feelings yet she had been wronged by Frank and was likely to be angry. She accepted the imposed shame from Frank and attempted to get relief from the shame by reconnecting through a denial of her experience and denying what had just happened. Frank's difficulty with giving specific examples might suggest that his reactions were primarily unresolved emotions rather than an objective grievance. He might be defending against the pain of his shame and his personal responsibility by imposing shame on her. The pastor responded well by making a mental note of this.

"Frank, has Susan told you about the two discussions I have had with her? Did she explain what we talked about?" asked Joe.

"Yes, we talked a little bit about it. I'm not sure I understand."

"Have you read the book about guilt and shame that Susan offered you?" Frank looked annoyed with the question and mumbled that he had looked through it. Joe continued. "Let me ask you—are you willing to do some work to understand Susan right now?"

"Sure, I guess so," Frank replied somewhat half-heartedly.

Commentary: The pastor was assessing Frank's willingness to be vulnerable before proceeding, as people only connect at a point of vulnerability. Frank's response would provide some extra sense of safety for Susan.

"I'll tell you right now, it's the measure of what kind of love you have for your spouse—your willingness to try and understand." Frank nodded and took Susan's hand.

"In a nutshell, Frank, Susan came to me because she was beginning to feel like she wasn't coping very well. She had lots of spiritual questions, and questions about her relationships with just about everybody. We've talked in particular about the issues of guilt and shame. In the interest of time, let me give you a summary of what we've talked about." Joe went on for a few minutes giving Frank a thumbnail sketch of the issues, and what his observations were about Susan in particular. "So Susan is trying to own any moral shame that is proper for her to bear, but also to get out from under some imposed shame that has come her way over the years. Does this make sense to you?"

"Well, sure, but how long do you think this is going to go on?"

Commentary: Joe had noted Frank's half-hearted response and continued to remain at a cognitive level. As he was describing the issues, he continued to assess not only Frank's capacity to empathize with his wife but also made eye contact with Susan in an attempt to remain connected with her and provide her a means to release shame. Frank responded to Joe's question by further imposing shame. The pastor then responded to both of them, keeping in mind that he would have to navigate carefully between Susan's issues and Frank's issues, avoiding getting too many out on the table at once.

"I think Susan has already gained some new insights that are going to immediately help. But one thing you must understand is that these are really lifelong issues. It's just part of life. We transgress, and, if things are working right, we feel moral shame. Then, once again someone comes along and tries to manipulate us into doing something by making us think we are guilty, and we have to deal with that. And there's always the issue of natural shame. We all have to face up to our limitations and the frailty of our lives, and have a good dose of humility." It was obvious to Joe that Frank was thinking hard about something. "Let me turn the tables for a minute, Frank. How do you think these issues apply to you?"

Commentary: The pastor attempted to engage Frank. He realized that he must not get too many different issues out at once, but sensed that he should respond to Frank's expressed need. As a pastoral counselor, Joe chose to further investigate Frank's situation and in doing so, Frank allowed himself to become a bit more vulnerable.

Frank paused a long time, then cleared his throat a couple of times before speaking. "I know I have to admit that not everything is Susan's fault. Sometimes I don't know why I do what I do. I suppose I deal with guilt differently than she does."

"What do you mean?"

"I've never had a very strong sense of guilt about anything. I just don't feel it. Every now and then that bothers me. Like last week, I guess I was a bit rough on my secretary. She tried to hide that she was crying but I could see from my office—and it's not the first time—and I said to myself, *What a jerk I am. But why doesn't this bother me more? Why don't I change?"*

"Those are some very important thoughts."

"I know, but it doesn't go any further than that. I have to tell you, sometimes when I'm sitting in church I feel like the biggest hypocrite. I guess if I'm honest I should tell you that that's why you see me here only occasionally these days."

Pastor Newquist continued to draw out of Frank concrete instances of when Frank's conscience bothered him, and what he did with those reactions. A picture emerged of a man very much running in fear from his own shame accumulated over many years. Pastor Newquist concentrated on Frank in the discussion, occasionally giving Susan eye contact and an opportunity to make comments. She seemed glad that Frank was talking openly.

"We've got a few more minutes, and we need to decide where to go from here," the pastor said.

Susan jumped in. "There's something else I'd like to bring up. Actually I wasn't going to, but . . . Frank and I have had some pretty serious arguments about his drinking patterns." Frank gave Susan a look of total disbelief. The pastor could see redness creeping up Frank's neck.

Susan continued. "I don't know when you label something a drinking problem, but I think we have a problem. There's too much drinking after work, too much on the weekend, too much on your business trips." Susan was now talking to Frank although he just looked straight ahead.

Commentary: The pastor had remained connected with Susan while showing Frank respect and empathy. Frank became more vulnerable and Susan's shame response sufficiently diminished so that she could reveal the secret.

Joe waited to see who would speak next. When the situation seemed practically frozen, Joe spoke. "Frank, do you have any response?"

"Yes, I do. I agreed to come in here to talk about Susan's problems, not to be attacked. Even if I do have a drink now and then, I think anyone could understand why." As he said this, he looked directly at Susan and she turned toward Joe.

Joe Newquist pursued this unexpected track in the session, asking Frank to consider the possibility that sometimes his drinking had gotten him into trouble. He identified that Susan was not responsible for Frank's decision to drink, labeled Susan's reported shame response as imposed shame, and stated that Frank was responsible for his use of alcohol. At the end of the session Joe told Frank that no matter how he defined it, his drinking was a problem in that it was an obvious source of tensions within their marriage. He left Frank with the strong recommendation that he set up an evaluation with a professional, although he wondered whether there was any chance Frank would follow through. He also wondered what this confrontation would mean for Susan in the days to come.

Joe called Susan the next day to see how things were going. Susan reported that "things have been very quiet around here." Joe then set up an appointment with Susan for the following week.

Session 4

When Joe Newquist called Susan to see how things were going after their last session, Susan seemed anxious to set up another appointment. She told the pastor that things were happening very fast in her thinking and she wanted to talk. Joe wondered whether the pastoral counseling was helping Susan get her feet on the ground so that she would have more of what she needed to work out issues of guilt or shame in her life or whether whole new avenues were opening up, which would warrant her being referred on for professional counseling. He made up his mind that he would reserve judgment on the question until their next meeting.

It appeared as though Frank was not at all inclined to have his drinking habits evaluated by anybody, but another set of circumstances forced Frank into it. Two days after the meeting of the couple and the pastor Frank had come back to work after lunch drunk and his boss had called him on the carpet. Frank had to agree to an evaluation through the company's health plan. Pastor Newquist decided to hold off on deciding how to follow up on Frank until after his evaluation. His hope was that Frank would be confronted with his drinking problem and would have a sense of moral shame that may open doors for some pastoral counsel. The pastor also decided that, in the meantime, the counseling with Susan should not be interrupted.

"So, what's been happening in your household in the past couple of weeks?" Joe asked Susan.

"Beyond what I told you on the phone about Frank's incident at work, a lot has been happening with us, and in me."

"Tell me about it."

"Frank just kind of closed down for the first couple of days. A lot of tension and anger in the air. He accused me of ambushing him and trying to blame my problems on him. But since the incident at work he has seemed very sheepish. I think he got really frightened, looking at the prospect of losing his job."

"That must have been very hard for you." Susan nodded in apparent agreement. Joe continued. "Since we've been talking about guilt and shame, how do you think those principles apply to Frank?"

"I think I see things much more clearly these days. For years Frank has been blaming me for just about everything that goes wrong for him. And I've taken it. I wonder now whether that did either him or me any good. Not that I'm unwilling to accept responsibility for my own failings. I know that I've been guilty of taking the easy way sometimes and getting what I want through trickery or manipulation."

"What are you saying now that you wouldn't have in the past?"

"I think that I've been operating for years as if I were the good wife by always taking the blame—I guess I saw it as helping my husband with his burden—while all the time I was really bitter inside and looked for ways in which I could get at him in some underhanded way."

"Where should the moral shame be felt in this whole situation?"

"I hope, I really hope, that Frank will own up to his drinking problem. Having remorse about that would be a whole new thing for him, so I'm not at all sure what's going to happen." Susan paused and thought for a moment. "As for me, I've been feeling moral shame for the ways in which I may have helped to perpetuate the problems of others. I shouldn't have just acted like a chameleon all these years, adapting to what everybody else wanted me to do and be."

Commentary: Joe attempted to form an empathetic connection with Susan and then help her identify the form of shame she was experiencing. Frank's withdrawal (i.e., disconnection) from her was likely to impose further shame, although Pastor Newquist noticed that she seemed not to have been greatly affected by his passive aggression, a good sign. Joe directed the discussion toward determining who was responsible for the guilt. It is necessary to determine who is responsible for the disconnection before the shame can be resolved.

"How did you learn how to do that?"

"Oh, I'm sure I developed that skill because of my mother's constant criticism. I see now that my two brothers didn't even bother. They just checked out." Joe thought that Susan's analytical thinking must have slowed down for a moment as a look of sadness and pain came over her face. "I know now that I can't keep going down the same track. It's just too exhausting. I also know I'm guilty of doing wrong things in order to make other people happy. I've lied for Frank, I've lied to my Christian friends by showing a facade of contentment and happiness. There are times I realize now when one of them tried to share their burdens with me, but because I appeared to be so invincible, they felt like they couldn't. I even wonder if Judy might not have gone into her depression if she hadn't kept trying to imitate me."

Commentary: Susan's experience is common. As people defend against their experience of imposed shame, they increase the use of their defenses, which leads to decreased vulnerability. Being less vulnerable, connection becomes more difficult and disconnection more probable. Thus, in an attempt to hide their experience of shame, they feel more shame. At this point of the session, Susan focused primarily on her moral shame. She had not yet accessed her anger regarding the imposition of shame on her.

"When you first came in to talk you speculated that what was bothering you was your 'secret,' as you called it—the fact that you were pregnant when you got married. What are your thoughts about that now?"

"I do feel moral shame about that. But now that's just part of the whole scene. I can see that my guilt there was also linked to my chameleon behavior. I compromised my standards in order to be like our friends. But that's really the story of my life."

"It sounds like you and your conscience have been doing overtime. Do you see how these different experiences get mixed up with each other? Because of the threat of imposed shame we turn around and do things that are wrong and end up having to deal with moral shame as well. Your guilt in being sexually active before marriage has been resolved and forgiven. Yet I still see you bearing most of the responsibility yourself. Tell me where you see imposed shame figuring into your life."

"It's almost like there are scenes in my mind that, when I think of them, I get that suffocating feeling that I think is imposed shame. I think of my mother calling me stupid, or getting mad at me and not talking to me for a whole day or two—good grief, ignore your own kid for a couple of days! I think of Frank sitting at the dinner table with his cocktail complaining about everything in the day and then somehow linking it with how I was in the morning, or what I fixed for dinner. It's not right, it's just not right."

"Listen Susan, any reasonable person would agree with you. Your anger is appropriate. Those things aren't right. And it's very important for you to get more and more discerning in order to be able to move on in your life."

"But even in saying those things I feel ashamed."

"The shame you feel is due to the disconnection, a kind of binding together of the feeling of anger with shame. What happened as a child when you were angry?"

"I never dared show my anger—my mother wouldn't talk to me for days if I did."

"Well, that's consistent too, isn't it? To be honest resulted in disconnection and the deep shame feelings. It turns into a vicious cycle: you get trapped in the expectations of others, and you don't dare resist because it might upset the apple cart and you would think yourself guilty."

Commentary: As they explored the imposed shame, Susan began to express her anger and revealed an anger-shame bind that had inhibited her resolution of both anger and shame. Joe validated her anger and would continue to explore imposed shame resolution.

"So what's the solution?"

"I think you've already begun to experience the solution. It goes by many names, many biblical categories. The biblical view of truth, for instance, implies that we should always strive to see things as they are. It does us no good to gloss over someone else's guilty actions in order to be 'nice.' Then, we just end up being guilty of tampering with truth. Then there's righteousness. What does 'righteousness' mean to you?"

"It's being right, doing right, all because of Christ's righteousness given to us."

"True enough. But now apply that principle to your relationships. Righteousness implies that we stand for what is right. When someone does something that stinks, we're not supposed to like it or accept it. Righteousness implies not only that I strive to do what is right, but that I look at my world with a discerning eye and not accept things done by others that are not right. If you were a witness to a child being mistreated, what would your reaction be?"

"I'd be very upset, I'd be angry."

"Right, and that's your sense of righteousness pointing you in the direction of moral order. The same things have to apply to the way people treat you. You need to establish boundaries with those who impose shame, with both Frank and your mother. For example, the next time your mother brings up the conditions that surrounded your marriage, you could say, 'Mom, I asked God for for-giveness, and I believe I am forgiven. I don't want to talk about this further.'"

Susan looked confused and asked, "But didn't Jesus allow him-self to be mistreated?"

"Yes he did, but that doesn't mean that the perpetrators 'got away with it.' Jesus was a victim and he willingly bore our shame, but he never was confused about who was guilty. I'm not saying you or any of us ought to lash out at someone who mistreats you, but on the other hand, you can't let shame be imposed on you so that you get morally, spiritually, and emotionally confused all the time."

Joe continued by showing Susan some biblical passages about truth and righteousness to illustrate his point. He did a similar thing with the biblical concepts of judgment and love, pointing out that all of these can and must work together in the Christian. As God's truth, righteousness, and judgment do not detract from his love, so in the Christian there can be a convergence of truth and grace. He also reminded Susan that all shame feels similar yet each type is resolved differently.

Commentary: For those who experience imposed shame, identi-fying the truth regarding who is responsible is often feared. To believe that someone else is guilty may upset that person and produce fur-ther disconnection. Even to think so is threatening to many as they fear being abandoned or judged by the other person. At times of feel-ing shame, it is often necessary to connect with another person in order to accurately attribute responsibility and identify the type of shame.

It was obvious to Joe that over the past weeks many lights had come on for Susan. She was at a point now of having enough of the pieces of the puzzle together that she could identify the whole pic-ture. Joe told Susan that they would meet one more time; he sched-uled a time in three weeks, and told her that he would like her to reread the small book on guilt and shame. She was asked to make a list of examples of times when she had felt shame as well as any questions that she had. He also told her he would follow up with Frank and see how he was doing.

Commentary: Joe provided Susan with a structure for assessing her experience that would lead to resolution of her shame response. She was instructed to list five columns on a page of paper and title them as follows: event, feelings, who's responsible, feelings, and action/resolution. Using this strategy, an individual can identify not only his or her feelings but also the object of the feelings and decide what needs to change in order to resolve the feelings. Consistent with the goals of Strategic Pastoral Counseling, this assignment is intended to be a tool clients can use over time to strengthen their coping abilities. Joe decided that at this time there was no reason to refer Susan on for more counseling. He might watch carefully over the next six months to make sure things progress. The pastoral counseling has already entered the disengagement stage.

Session 5:
The Disengagement Stage

Session 5

Susan told the pastor how much she had appreciated his meeting with her (adding a predictable "with your busy schedule"). She said that she knew that their discussions were already making a tremendous difference for her. Frank had been told by the alcohol abuse counselor that his behavior certainly did amount to an unhealthy dependence on drinking and he agreed to participate in their program. Susan said she wasn't completely sure whether it was to please his boss or because he really wanted to. She would wait and see what happened after the program. Things had actually been better than civil around the house.

Joe affirmed Susan in her approach to Frank's issues and said he had a good talk with Frank on the phone and would stay in touch with him. Joe also asked how their children were doing during these difficult times. Susan said that she had decided to spend more time with them doing simple things that they liked to do, trying to make the home environment more relaxed. She had the most concerns about her oldest daughter who, at sixteen, was already quite a private person. When Susan had attempted to have a heart-to-heart talk about the situation concerning her dad, the daughter was basically unwilling to talk.

Commentary: As imposed shame is resolved, people are able to see others, to be sensitive to the needs and feelings of others, and to set appropriate boundaries. Joe began the session by listening to Susan and providing support for how she had coped and the decisions she had made, all of which facilitated deeper connection. He continued to assess her understanding of guilt and shame, her acceptance of her own emotional reactions, and her current attributions of responsibility.

"I fear that there are going to be hard times ahead," Susan said. "Don't misunderstand me, I'm very glad to understand myself better, but in a way I feel like my eyes are open wider and I see more cracks than ever before."

Joe shook his head in agreement. "Yes, having lived with much imposed shame is very difficult. I think you're giving a perfect description of natural shame, Susan. When all is said and done, all of us need to take a good hard look at ourselves and realize that we are still human, 'we have this treasure in clay vessels,' as Paul said. That means we're limited, we're fallible, and we're frail."

"I'm afraid of messing up. I'm afraid of changing, but I'm also afraid of being the same."

Joe leaned forward, made eye contact, and said, "Yes, that's natural shame. Think of it this way. God has called us to a life of faith. That doesn't mean life without doubts or without fears. Faith wouldn't be faith if we had what we hoped for. Paul said that too. Fear and doubt are opportunities for faith. Natural shame is an attitude of humility that will safeguard the way in which we appropriate God's solutions to our problems."

"I'm not sure I understand."

"Well, have you ever known someone who had an answer for a serious life problem that seemed just too easy? Maybe someone who thought their shaky marriage would be solved by having a child or joining the choir. Maybe Frank's looking for a quick and easy solution to your family's problems."

"Sure, I can think of plenty of others, too."

"If those people had a realistic picture of what they were up against, and if they weren't hanging onto their naive optimism, they might look at real solutions to their problems. That's what natural shame can do for us. It's not hopelessness, but realism that allows us to find real and workable solutions rather than quick fixes that don't work."

"So it's okay if I feel a little shaky about the future?"

"Yes, it's okay. That's the way it is. It's a perfectly understandable—and realistic—attitude for someone who has come through a lot of confusion and distress and who is facing significant changes. And remember, it doesn't mean you don't have faith. Faith is holding onto God when you yourself feel shaky."

Commentary: Joe remained connected with Susan through an acceptance of her feelings and assisting her in identifying her feelings. Nonverbal connections such as leaning forward and eye contact are just as important. Understanding often provides an increase in self-acceptance and trust and a decrease in fear and shame.

"Can't God work a miracle? I mean, I know you've told us from the pulpit many times that change is usually a process, but I know that you also believe in miracles. Why can't I ask for perfect faith and an instant change in me or Frank or my mother or all of us?"

"Sure, God can and does work miracles. We ought to pray for his intervention and his life-changing power. But he may choose different ways of accomplishing that. God's working in us over time is a miracle, too. God can work instant change, but obviously he chooses a different way much of the time. I suppose someday we'll realize why God chose to put such emphasis on the process of growth. Look at the way he chose to make human beings as creatures that move from infancy to maturity."

Commentary: It is common for people to want to avoid the pain of accepting responsibility or holding others responsible and they often need reassurance that it is okay to feel pain, that change takes time and rarely occurs instantly, and that God will never disconnect or abandon them in the process. Shame resolution is a lifetime process. For those who have lived with much imposed shame, it is novel to think that it is safe and permissible to accept our inadequacies, our imperfections, and the imperfections of others.

"In a way it seems like a sudden change has already occurred for me. I'm just looking at so many things differently than I was a few weeks ago. I feel freed up, and I don't feel like I'm on a treadmill. I'm a whole lot more confident about coping with things."

Joe and Susan spent the rest of the time talking about practical issues. He reviewed her need to continue to use her new understandings and coping tools in resolving her shame. How could she be helpful in Frank's treatment? Should she continue with all the things she had been doing in the church? Should she seek a confidante with whom to share on a regular basis? Joe strongly encouraged this. He told her he did not think that he would refer her on to professional counseling as long as she felt she was coping well, but he did think that she would greatly benefit by meeting every other week with a mature woman in the church who was familiar with the issues of guilt and shame and could pray with her and encourage her. In addition, he encouraged Susan to follow the recommendations offered in Frank's treatment, which might include her getting education and/or support on the issues surrounding alcohol abuse.

Commentary: In short-term counseling insights and understandings often lead to rapid changes in behavior. Long-term behavioral and self-esteem changes require consistent and persistent implementation of the new insights, understandings, and coping tools. The pastor might have further emphasized this to assist Susan in maintaining realistic expectations. Understanding and insight are often necessary but not sufficient to resolve the shame experience. Connection with God and another person are required and Joe provided a means for Susan to continue to have this. As she did not display indications of significant impairment in her ability to function in her daily activities, Joe correctly concluded that she did not need professional help.

Pastor Newquist told Susan that though he would not be setting up another pastoral counseling appointment with her, he wanted to hear in a month or so how things were going. He left her with a verse—"we set our hearts at rest in his presence whenever our hearts condemn us. For God is greater than our hearts" (1 John 3:19–21)— and spent time praying for her and all of the people who had figured into their talks.

Commentary: This final session provided many evidences that Susan was no longer under the suffocating effects of imposed shame and had some confidence that she could distinguish between guilt and shame and resolve both. She had confirmed with Pastor Newquist what she thought she had worked out years ago, that God had indeed forgiven her for the guilt of premarital sexual activity. While much had changed, many areas of her life remained in transition. The termination of the counseling relationship occurred with Susan displaying a greater acceptance of herself, a reduction in the distress she felt, and an increased comfort with and love for God. She could now venture into new relationships with a capacity to honestly share herself with others. Many experiences of imposed shame result in much greater impairment in daily functioning than was evident in Susan. Clinical depression, thoughts of suicide, anxiety, identity confusion, sleep disturbances, disorders of sexual functioning, and eating disorders all may have their roots in unresolved shame and guilt. While these problems may present challenges outside the scope of the expertise and available time of the pastoral counselor, these individuals may still benefit greatly from Strategic Pastoral Counseling, either before or concurrent with services from a mental health professional. God's love, acceptance, grace, and justice manifested in a human relationship can reinforce our connection with God and enhance our understanding of his nature and character and our own identity.

Epilogue

$\mathbf{I}$f the Christian church cannot or does not carefully address the issues of guilt and shame, who will?

The human race is universally affected by the fall; no one is unaffected by guilt and shame. Yet we see so many misguided ideas about the human condition. While the cultural crisis of vague relativism that tries to bury the very notion of guilt unfolds in our society, individuals continue to have the experience of shame. But what will they do with it?

The good news that the church bears to a lost world is that we can understand exactly what our problem is: we are a guilty race that senses shame as a consequence and that sometimes sinful human beings victimize others, but in Christ there is a complete solution to our debt and a process of healing the wounds of shame.

The church can carefully communicate that message through virtually all of its ministries of teaching, shepherding, and counseling. Biblical preaching, for instance, is not heaping shame on people's heads nor is it indiscretely absolving people of their moral responsibilities. Rather, it should systematically describe the careful distinctions the Scriptures themselves draw between real guilt and imagined guilt, shame that is proper or imposed. Churches are discovering more and more what forms of ministry like small groups can do to provide an accepting environment where sons and daughters of Adam and Eve can venture out of their hiding

167

places and join the community of God. Those same small groups may be the source of loving confrontation when a member needs to discover his or her own guilt and go through the process of sensing moral shame and seeking reconciliation.

And then there is pastoral counseling. Those who have been suspicious of its value or validity so often base their criticisms on the question of whether it minimizes personal responsibility and guilt. Biblically informed and psychologically sound counseling will do nothing of the sort. A proper synthesis of the two, which has been the aim of this book, will provide careful criteria for discerning where guilt really lies and why we experience shame in the many complex ways we do. The model described in this book and the examples used are an attempt at providing an integrative model of Christian belief and psychology. The psychological side is responsive to the theories and findings of affect theory, developmental theory, and cognitive-behavioral theories. Using this common ground, Strategic Pastoral Counseling can be the decisive moment when individuals are liberated from their guilt or shame.

Appendix

A Handout: What Are Guilt and Shame?

Guilt is the objective state of being responsible for a wrongdoing or transgression. Guilt is not an emotion or feeling; rather, guilt is the status of being in the wrong. Its opposite is innocence. Guilt is independent of my experience. For example, I may be guilty and not be aware of my guilt or I may believe that I am guilty and actually be innocent.

Shame is the subjective, personal, and painful emotional experience that occurs when one feels disconnected. It is a painful awareness of feeling inadequate, unworthy, and exposed. When we feel shame, we often feel inhibited, or to some degree, like we want to hide. Although all shame feels essentially the same, shame has three distinct forms.

Moral shame is the sense of remorse or shame felt when I judge that I am responsible for a transgression or wrongdoing, when I am responsible for some disconnection. God uses moral shame to help us identify the wrongdoing, know limits, and facilitate reconnection with the person who has been wronged. It is what we mean when we speak of having a bad conscience.

Imposed shame is a sense of shame that is imposed by one person on another. Someone else is causing the disconnection. Imposed shame may feel the same as moral shame yet has a different cause, namely, someone else's behavior. The intent of the other person is not relevant to the experience of imposed shame. Some situations in which imposed shame may occur include the denial of responsibility or misattribution of responsibility by another, abandonment or neglect by another, or in situations of emotional, mental, physical, or sexual abuse. Repeated imposed shame over time can profoundly affect a person.

Natural shame is the sense of being fallible, limited, or frail. It is a result of the disconnection between the human race and God because of the fall and the resulting sin nature. We experience natural shame when we sense that we are unable to be perfect, and may not be known fully or understood by others. We may sense natural shame at times of reflection and in situations in which no specific transgression has occurred and no specific person is responsible for the disconnection. The humility of realizing our natural limitations is important to living responsible and safe lives.

The Resolution of Shame and Guilt

Shame is resolved when a reconnection occurs. While all shame feels similar, the type of shame can be identified by the following question: Who is responsible for the disconnection?

If I am responsible for the disconnection, then I am feeling moral shame. Moral shame is resolved through dealing with guilt and the reconnection with the one who was wronged. Moral shame resolution involves:

- acceptance of personal responsibility
- ownership and resolution of the other emotional reactions involved in the situation

- confession of the wrongdoing
- acceptance of forgiveness from the other, God, and self
- restitution or correction as is relevant in the situation

If another person is responsible for the disconnection, then the experience of shame is imposed shame. Imposed shame resolution involves the following steps:

- reattribution of responsibility, that is, holding the proper person responsible for his or her actions and accepting responsibility for my own actions
- identification, ownership, and resolution of all emotional reactions in the situation
- use of anger to reestablish ego-boundaries
- acceptance of love from another person
- application of love to oneself
- confrontation of the other person (either in person or symbolically)
- confession of personal responsibility
- acceptance of forgiveness from God, the other person, and oneself
- rebuilding the relationship in truth

If no specific transgression has occurred and my humanness is responsible for the disconnection, then the experience is natural shame. Natural shame is resolved through acceptance of God's reconnection with us through Jesus Christ and our acceptance of redemption and grace.

References

Alonso, A., and S. Rutan. 1988. Shame and guilt in psychotherapy supervision. *Psychotherapy* 25(4): 576–81.

Benner, D. G. 1992. *Strategic pastoral counseling: A short-term structured model.* Grand Rapids: Baker.

Bradshaw, John. 1988. *Bradshaw on: The family.* Deerfield Beach, Fla.: Health Communications.

Broucek, F. J. 1991. *Shame and the self.* New York: Guilford.

Brown, H. M. 1991. Shame and relapse issues with the chemically dependent client. *Alcoholism Treatment Quarterly* 8(3): 77–82.

Clapp, R. 1991. Shame crucified. *Christianity Today* 34(3): 26–28.

Darley, J. M., and T. R. Shultz. 1990. Moral rules: Their content and acquisition. *Annual Review of Psychology* 41:525–56.

Frank, E. S. 1991. Shame and guilt in eating disorders. *American Journal of Orthopsychiatry* 61(2): 303–6.

Harper, J. M., and M. H. Hoopes. 1990. *Uncovering shame.* New York: W. W. Norton.

Karen, R. 1992. Shame. *Atlantic* 269(2): 40–70.

Kaufman, G. 1985. *Shame: The power of caring.* Rochester, Vt.: Schenkman.

———. 1989. *The psychology of shame.* New York: Springer.

Nathanson, D. L. 1987. A timetable for shame. In *The many faces of shame,* ed. D. L. Nathanson, 1–62. New York: Guilford.

———. 1992. *Shame and pride: Affect, sex, and the birth of the self.* New York: W. W. Norton.

Osherson., S., and S. Krugman. 1990. Men, shame, and psychotherapy. *Psychotherapy* 27(3): 327–39.

Pauck, Wilhelm, trans. and ed. 1961. Martin Luther's *Lectures on Romans*. Philadelphia: Westminster.

Potter-Efron, P. S. 1987. Creative approaches to shame and guilt: Helping the adult child of an alcoholic. *Alcoholism Treatment Quarterly* 4(2): 39–56.

Spero, M. H. 1984. Shame: An object-relational formulation. *Psychoanalytic Study of the Child* 39:259–82.

Tomkins, S. S. 1962. *Affect, imagery, consciousness: The positive affects.* Vol. 1. New York: Springer.

———. 1963. *Affect, imagery, consciousness: The negative affects.* Vol. 2. New York: Springer.

———. Affect theory. In *Approaches to emotion,* ed. K. R. Scherer and R. Ekman, 163–95. Hillsdale, N.J.: Erlbaum.

———. 1987. Shame. In *The many faces of shame,* ed. D. L. Nathanson, 133–61. New York: Guilford.

Tournier, Paul. *Guilt and grace: A psychological study.* New York: Harper, 1962.